Laravel 11 Cookbook

Proven workflows, solutions and techniques to build, deploy, and monitor Laravel applications

Sanya Voltra

Published by: GitforGits

Publisher: Sonal Dhandre

www.gitforgits.com

support@gitforgits.com

Printed in India

First Printing: February 2025

ISBN: 978-93-49174-35-1

Cover Design by: Kitten Publishing

Prologue

I cannot forget the first time I discovered PHP's incredible power. It was amazing to see static pages transform into living, breathing applications! As frameworks came and went, one name rose to the top—Laravel. Its elegant syntax, intuitive structure, and vibrant ecosystem transformed everyday development into an inspired craft. Laravel 11 is here, and it's better than ever! I can't wait to show you what it can do.

I'm Sanya Voltra, and I've built my career solving the puzzles that emerge when code and real-world demands collide. In this book, I invite you to walk beside me through each challenge and solution, recipe by recipe. This will allow you to set up a rock-solid Linux environment tuned for Laravel, from installing PHP 8.0 and Composer to locking down file permissions and integrating the tools you rely on every day. And the best part? You'll gain confidence the moment your first artisan command runs without error. Once you start, you'll be amazed at how easy it is to craft dynamic routes that adapt to user input. And you'll love how you can organize CRUD operations with resource controllers to keep your code clean and maintainable. We will fortify your application's defenses—implementing login systems, role-based access checks, social authentication, and two-factor verification—so that every request arrives from someone you trust.

Next, we're going to create a model of your data using Eloquent relationships that reflect real-world connections. We'll also manage schema changes through migrations and seed lifelike test data for development. When queries slow your pages, you'll be able to apply eager loading and indexing techniques to restore speed and scalability.

As you apply server-side rules, build custom checks, and centralize exception responses, you'll find that data validation and error handling become second nature. You will be thrilled to see errors logged and alerted in real time with tools already at your fingertips, so you'll never miss a thing. And you'll never have to worry about heavy tasks blocking your users again! You'll be able to dispatch jobs into background queues, configure retry logic for transient failures, and schedule routine operations—backups, report generation, cache refreshes—so they run like clockwork. Your media files will live on secure disks, automatically resized and optimized, then streamed and downloaded efficiently even under traffic spikes.

Every recipe in this book is a building block for another, and each one is more exciting than the last! You'll never repeat steps you've already mastered; instead, you'll revisit and extend your work, gaining both depth and momentum. You'll walk away with a toolkit of patterns and commands that you can apply to any Laravel project, and you can trust them to get the job done. This book tackles the scenarios that emerge in day-to-day development—the migrations that fail, the N+1 queries that creep in, the authentication gaps, the slow batch jobs, the overlooked backups—and equips you with ready solutions. While it doesn't claim to cover every aspect of Laravel, it does provide you with the tried-and-true methods you need to keep your applications running like a dream and your focus where it belongs — on the features that will delight your users.

I absolutely can't wait to show you what Laravel 11 can do! Let's dive in and turn challenges into opportunities. By the time you reach the final recipe, you'll have a much deeper understanding of Laravel's inner workings. You'll be so confident that you'll be able to build, troubleshoot, and maintain sophisticated applications with ease!

Content

Preface

This book is an incredible resource for PHP developers! It's packed with hands-on recipes that will empower you to overcome any real-world challenge you face when building, debugging, and deploying Laravel applications. You'll start by installing PHP 8.0, Composer, setting file permissions, and integrating tools like PhpStorm and Laravel Debugbar. Next, there are so many advanced routing and controller patterns to explore, from dynamic URL parameters to resource controllers and custom JSON APIs. You'll be amazed at how your application responds precisely to user requests. For security, you'll implement Laravel Breeze for user authentication, craft role-based access controls with middleware, add social logins via Socialite, and enforce two-factor authentication with Fortify, hardening your application against unauthorized access. Then, you'll get to define Eloquent models and relationships, manage migrations, and seed realistic test data. You'll also be able to optimize queries using eager loading to eliminate performance bottlenecks.

With server-side validation, you can rest assured that your data is always accurate and reliable. Plus, you can create custom validation rules with clear feedback, centralize exception handling in Handler.php, and set up real-time error monitoring with Laravel Pulse. You'll also learn to automate critical workflows—configuring queue drivers and background jobs, retrying failed tasks, scheduling recurring operations, and backing up databases and media—freeing your team from manual maintenance. Next, you will be able to carry out file storage and media handling. You will configure secure local disks, process and optimize images with Intervention Image, and implement chunked streaming and secure downloads. Once you do, you'll be able to automate analytical reporting, from custom shell scripts to scheduled generation of performance-insight summaries. And you'll tie it all into Laravel's Scheduler and Linux cron.

In this book, you'll find ready-to-use solutions to the scenarios you face day to day. Whether you're dealing with broken migrations, N+1 queries, authentication gaps, missing alerts, or sluggish jobs, this book has you covered. It addresses the most common pain points in Laravel development without claiming to cover every possible edge case. Instead, it gives you proven recipes that let you focus on building features, confident that you have reliable fixes at your fingertips.

In this book you will learn how to:

- Achieve mastery of the Linux-based Laravel setup: Let's dive into the world of PHP installation, Composer, file permissions, and IDE configuration!
- Build dynamic routes, resource controllers, and Blade views for robust request handling.
- Protect your applications with Breeze authentication, role-based middleware, Socialite logins, and two factor auth.
- Discover the magic of Eloquent models, one-to-many and many-to-many relationships, migrations, and seed realistic test data.

- Optimize database performance using eager loading, selective column queries, and proper indexing strategies.
- Take advantage of server-side validation, custom rules, and centralized exception handling for unparalleled data integrity.
- Keep an eye on errors in real time with the amazing Laravel Pulse, Debugbar, and Telescope dashboards.
- Offload your heavy tasks with ease using job queues, retry strategies, and Laravel Scheduler automation.
- Securely store, process, resize, and stream media using Laravel filesystem and Intervention Image.
- Automate backups, generate analytical reports, and integrate custom shell scripts with Laravel commands.

GitforGits

Prerequisites

This book is fr Laravel developers, PHP programmers, and Web Developers who are curiously looking out for PHP and Laravel solutions that can help them to troubleshoot and debug their webn applications. Prior knowledge of Laravel framework is sufficient to take this book ahead.

Codes Usage

Are you in need of some helpful code examples to assist you in your programming and documentation? Look no further! Our book offers a wealth of supplemental material, including code examples and exercises.

Not only is this book here to aid you in getting your job done, but you have our permission to use the example code in your programs and documentation. However, please note that if you are reproducing a significant portion of the code, we do require you to contact us for permission.

But don't worry, using several chunks of code from this book in your program or answering a question by citing our book and quoting example code does not require permission. But if you do choose to give credit, an attribution typically includes the title, author, publisher, and ISBN. For example, "Laravel 11 Cookbook by Sanya Voltra".

If you are unsure whether your intended use of the code examples falls under fair use or the permissions outlined above, please do not hesitate to reach out to us at support@gitforgits.com.

We are happy to assist and clarify any concerns.

Acknowledgement

I owe a tremendous debt of gratitude to GitforGits, for their unflagging enthusiasm and wise counsel throughout the entire process of writing this book. Their knowledge and careful editing helped make sure the piece was useful for people of all reading levels and comprehension skills. In addition, I'd like to thank everyone involved in the publishing process for their efforts in making this book a reality. Their efforts, from copyediting to advertising, made the project what it is today.

Finally, I'd like to express my gratitude to everyone who has shown me unconditional love and encouragement throughout my life. Their support was crucial to the completion of this book. I appreciate your help with this endeavour and your continued interest in my career.

CHAPTER 1: SETTING UP PHP AND LARAVEL ENVIRONMENT

Overview

In this chapter, we will walk through setting up a Linux-based development environment just for Laravel 11. We will start by updating your Linux system and installing PHP 8.0 along with its required extensions. Then, set up Composer to manage your dependencies and install Laravel version 11, which will help keep your project framework organized. We will learn how to set up important environment variables and create an application key for security.

We will also learn about the importance of Laravel's directory layout and how to manage file permissions to keep things secure and running smoothly. We will also get a solid set of tools for development, like PhpStorm, Laravel Debugbar, and Telescope. These will make your workflow and debugging process better. Finally, we will set up Git version control, create commit conventions, and configure remote repositories to enable seamless collaboration with your team. It'll give you all the essential skills you need to get started in Laravel development with confidence and precision.

Recipe 1: Installing PHP 8 and Laravel 11 using Composer

You work in a lively office where a new Linux server was just delivered to our team. The system is totally barebones—no PHP, Composer, or Laravel installed—and you are all set to dive in and get everything up and running. Today, we're laying the groundwork for an exciting project by installing PHP 8.0 as the base for Laravel 11.We will use Composer as our go-to dependency manager to fetch Laravel, configure essential environment variables, and then verify that everything's working. This live scenario is set up so that each step builds on the last one, getting you ready for a smooth transition into more advanced development tasks.

Installing PHP 8.0

Before diving into new installations, it's essential that you update your Linux server to ensure that every package is current. To do this, type in:

```
sudo apt update && sudo apt upgrade -y
```

The above command will synchronize your package listings with the latest repository data and upgrade any pre-installed packages. This step sets you up with a fresh system with no potential conflicts or errors in later installations.

Now our Laravel framework relies on PHP 8.0, so the next step is installing this version along with a set of critical extensions. These extensions will empower your application by handling string operations, XML parsing, network communications, and file compression.

To do this, simply run the following command:

```
sudo apt install php8.0 php8.0-common php8.0-cli php8.0-
mbstring php8.0-xml php8.0-curl php8.0-zip -y
```

After the installation, make sure everything is in place by checking the PHP version:

```
php -v
```

This command should display details about PHP 8.0 and confirms the right version installed.

Installing Composer

Now that PHP is installed, it's time to explore what Composer is? It is considered to be the perfect go-to tool for managing PHP dependencies, since it automatically handles the libraries needed for your project, saving you time and reducing manual errors. With Composer, you can effortlessly download and manage updates to Laravel and its required components.

So now, let's get this Composer on our Linux server. To do this, run:

```
curl -sS https://getcomposer.org/installer -o composer-
setup.php
```

This will download the Composer's installer script directly to your current directory. Once the download is complete, verify the integrity of the installer by comparing its hash to the one provided on Composer's official website.

After you've ensured the script is safe, run the installer with PHP:

```
php composer-setup.php --install-dir=/usr/local/bin --
filename=composer
```

This command places Composer in the **`/usr/local/bin`** directory, allowing you to call it from anywhere. Once Composer is installed, you can perform clean up by removing the installer file as below:

```
rm composer-setup.php
```

Finally, confirm that Composer is ready for action:

```
composer --version
```

This should output the Composer version, showing that it's correctly installed and available for use in your upcoming Laravel setup.

Installing Laravel 11

With PHP and Composer successfully installed, the next step is installing our most awaiting Laravel 11. Now to do this, we will create a new project directory, we will simply name it "myapp" and will run the following Composer command:

```
composer create-project --prefer-dist laravel/laravel myapp
"11.*"
```

What this does is, it instructs Composer to fetch Laravel version 11 along with all its dependencies. The command not only downloads the required packages but also organizes your project directory with folders like **app**, **config**, **database**, and **resources**.

Next, after the command completes, move into your new project directory:

```
cd myapp
```

Here, we will notice Laravel's standard structure is already in place—this is your playground for developing everything from basic routes to complex business logic. Each folder has its purpose, which makes the development process more intuitive as you continue to build and enhance your application.

Configuring Environment Variables and Verifying Installation

Setting up Environment File

The Laravel framework comes with a sample environment configuration file named **.env.example**. We need to customize this file to match our specific Linux setup. To do this, simply copy the example to create a usable **.env** file:

```
cp .env.example .env
```

Your new **.env** file will store critical settings like database credentials, mail configurations, and the application key. This separation of configuration from the codebase is essential as you begin to add more functionality and eventually move into production.

Generating Unique Application Key

A unique application key secures your encrypted data and user sessions. We can generate this key using the Laravel Artisan command:

```
php artisan key:generate
```

This command automatically updates your **.env** file with a newly generated key and confirms that the application is now secure. The key acts as a safeguard against vulnerabilities.

Verifying Laravel Setup

To ensure that everything is running smoothly, let's start the built-in Laravel development server using Artisan:

```
php artisan serve
```

This command launches a local development server, typically running at http://127.0.0.1:8000 which you can open in your web browser and navigate to this address. You should see Laravel's welcome page—this page is your first confirmation that the installation was successful and that your Linux server is now set up for Laravel development.

Recipe 2: Configuring Linux File Permissions and Directory Structure

Now that you've got PHP, Composer, and Laravel 11 set up on your Linux machine, like you did in the last recipe, it's time to move on. So, picture this. You've got this basic system set up for Laravel, and it's starting to get data and user interactions. In our busy office, we will get to work on a project, tweaking its structure and security by getting hands-on with the Linux file system. We will need to be able to confidently navigate the Laravel directory structure and learn essential Linux commands, like listing directories, managing ownership, and modifying file permissions. And when you get the hang of these concepts, we will not only be super-skilled in the practical stuff, but we will also be able to keep your Laravel project running smoothly and reliably.

Revisiting Laravel Project Structure

Before diving into permissions, let's refresh our understanding of the directory structure we created in the first recipe. To do this, first navigate to your project folder, "myapp":

```
cd myapp
```

Now, let's list the contents of the directory:

```
ls -l
```

We will see a well-organized layout with folders such as **app**, **bootstrap**, **config**, **database**, **public**, **resources**, **storage**, and **vendor**. We know that each folder plays a key role. For instance, the **storage** directory is where Laravel writes logs, caches, and files, while **bootstrap/cache** holds crucial cache files that improve performance. The recognition of these components is essential since, as your project evolves, these files and directories become critical for both functionality and security.

Checking Default Permissions

The file permissions on your Linux server dictate who can read, write, or execute your project files. To di this, simply run the following to see the permissions in your project:

```
ls -l
```

The subsequent output will show you details like **drwxr-xr-x** for each directory. In this notation, we will notice the three sets of permissions for the file owner, group, and others. It's important to note that for Laravel, certain directories, such as **storage** and **bootstrap/cache**, require write permissions for the web server.

Configuring Directory Permissions

Now, let's secure our Laravel project by ensuring that the web server can appropriately write to critical directories while maintaining a secure overall structure. In our Linux environment, the web server commonly runs under a specific user account such as **www-data**. This means that **storage** and **bootstrap/cache** must be owned by or accessible to this user for proper operation.

Changing Ownership

To do this, run the following command to change the owner and group recursively for the **storage** and **bootstrap/cache** directories:

```
sudo chown -R www-data:www-data storage bootstrap/cache
```

This command assigns **www-data** as both the owner and group for these directories, ensuring that files created by Laravel will have the correct access rights for the web server. This step is critical for both security and functionality, as improper permissions can lead to application errors.

Modifying Permissions

Next, let's update the directory permissions so that the owner and group have full read, write, and execute permissions, while others can read and execute only. Simply run the following command:

```
sudo chmod -R 775 storage bootstrap/cache
```

The permission code **775** guarantees that you (as part of the group) and the web server can modify files here, which is necessary for writing logs, caching data, or uploading files. It also blocks unauthorized modifications from other users on the system.

And, to ensure that these changes have been applied, you try to list the directories' details once more:

```
ls -l storage
ls -l bootstrap/cache
```

You should see permissions resembling **drwxrwxr-x** for these directories. This output confirms that your adjustments are in place, and both you and the web server can manage the files needed for optimal Laravel performance.

Laravel's Access to File System

It's important to be be well versed with how Laravel leverages these directories in our project. The **storage** directory is not merely a random folder; it's your central hub for dynamic content. It stores application logs in **storage/logs**, caches compiled views and configuration files in **storage/framework**, and even temporarily holds uploaded files. If you ever encounter issues related to caching or log generation, revisiting these permissions is often the first troubleshooting step.

Similarly, the **bootstrap/cache** directory is crucial during the application bootstrapping process. Laravel compiles configuration and route files into this directory to reduce overhead during request handling. If the web server cannot write to this directory because of strict permissions, you could face runtime errors or slower performance.

Practical Linux Commands

As you keep working on your Laravel application, we will be using these Linux commands over and over again. I'll give you a quick rundown of the main commands we will need:

- Listing Files and Directories

Use **ls -l** to check the file structure and permissions.

- Changing File Ownership

Use **chown** to set the correct owner for directories, ensuring your web server and development tools have the right access.

- Modifying Permissions

Use **chmod** to grant or restrict access according to your project's needs.

- Viewing Directory Trees

For a clearer view of your project's structure, consider installing the **tree** command:

```
sudo apt install tree
```

```
tree -L 2
```

If you get the hang of these Linux commands, we will be able to troubleshoot and maintain your Laravel project more effectively as new challenges pop up. As we progress together, every new command and configuration builds naturally on what you've already mastered. This incremental learning process is designed to boost your confidence and equip you with practical skills that will be essential for each subsequent phase of your Laravel development adventure on Linux.

Recipe 3: Configuring Linux Tools for Laravel

Now that you've successfully installed Laravel 11 and got the hang of its file structure and permissions on your Linux system, it's time to take things up a notch by setting up a suite of development tools that'll streamline your daily workflow. Just picture our team kicking off a new project meeting where everyone's pumped to see how a solid development environment can crank up productivity. In your development station, we will be able to set up essential tools like PhpStorm for an IDE with lots of features, Laravel Debugbar for debugging in real time, and Laravel Telescope for advanced monitoring. And when you are ready to dive into more advanced topics like debugging and performance analysis, these tools will be there for you.

Setting up PhpStorm

PhpStorm is a powerful IDE that provides intelligent code assistance and debugging features, perfect for Laravel development. There are a couple of ways to install PhpStorm on Linux, but using Snap simplifies the process.

To begin, just execute:

```
sudo snap install phpstorm --classic
```

This will install PhpStorm with classic confinement, ensuring that all the necessary system privileges are granted. Once installed, launch PhpStorm from your application menu or by typing:

```
phpstorm
```

After starting PhpStorm, you are prompted to configure initial settings like themes, keymaps, and plugins. Now here, make sure that you install the recommended plugins such as:

- **`Laravel Plugin`** (for Blade support, route navigation, etc.)
- **`PHP Intelephense`** (for code intelligence)

You can add these plugins via **`File > Settings > Plugins`**, then search for "Laravel" and "PHP Intelephense". The installation of these plugins ia simply DIY. After doing this, restart PhpStorm to activate the enhancements, asnd you will see that your IDE becomes a powerful extension of your Linux environment.

Installing Laravel Debugbar

The Laravel Debugbar is an indispensable tool during development. It provides a real-time overview of the application's internal processes, such as route handling, database queries, and log messages. This insight is especially useful as you continue to refine your application and track performance bottlenecks.

So, to integrate Debugbar into the project, navigate to your project directory and run:

```
cd myapp
composer require barryvdh/laravel-debugbar --dev
```

This command installs the Debugbar package as a development dependency. Once the package is installed, Laravel automatically registers the Debugbar service provider. You may check your **`config/app.php`** file if you want to verify the provider is loaded, though this is usually done automatically by Laravel's package auto-discovery feature.

Next, after installation, run your project server with:

```
php artisan serve
```

Then, browse to http://127.0.0.1:8000. You should see a new Debugbar panel at the bottom of your screen. This panel shows detailed insights about rendered views, executed queries, and processed middleware.

Setting up Laravel Telescope

The Laravel Telescope offers an advanced debugging and monitoring dashboard that records and displays information about every request entering your application. This tool not only complements Debugbar but also provides detailed log insights, making it easier for you to fine-tune your Laravel system as the project scales.

Now to install Telescope, run the following within your project directory:

```
composer require laravel/telescope --dev
```

Once installed, publish Telescope's configuration and assets with:

```
php artisan telescope:install
```

After publishing the assets, complete the installation by running your migrations:

```
php artisan migrate
```

The above commands set up Telescope's database tables and configuration settings. Once completed, start your Laravel server:

```
php artisan serve
```

Now, navigate to http://127.0.0.1:8000/telescope. We will see Telescope's dashboard populated with live data from your application. The interface allows you to inspect recent requests, exceptions, logs, and queries which gives a strong deep dive into your application's internals.

Integrating Essential Linux-Based Tools

While you might have already set up version control earlier, remember that Git is your steadfast companion in managing code changes. On Linux, you can always check the status of your repository using:

```
git status
```

For advanced Linux users, terminal multiplexers like **`tmux`** or **`screen`** allow you to run multiple sessions in one terminal window. Installing tmux is straightforward:

```
sudo apt install tmux -y
```

These tools let you split your terminal window and monitor several processes simultaneously. These tools become an asset as you juggle tasks like server logs, debugging sessions, and live code edits.

Recipe 4: Integrating Git into Laravel

Now that you have a fully functional Laravel 11 project on your Linux machine, you should make sure that every team member can collaborate effectively. In the shared development environment of your office, you need to set up a solid version control system for the project, which we've named "myapp." Git is the industry standard for version control, and it lets you track changes, maintain commit history, and sync code across multiple developers. In this recipe,we will walk you through setting up a Git repository in "myapp," setting up commit conventions, and configuring remote repositories—all using Linux terminal commands.

Initializing Git Repository

First, navigate into "myapp":

```
cd myapp
```

Then, initialize the Git by running:

```
git init
```

This command sets up a new Git repository in your project folder, creating a hidden **`.git`** directory where Git will store all version history and configuration settings.

Configuring Commit Conventions

Creating .gitignore File

Before adding files to your repository, it's important to tell Git which files or directories to exclude. Laravel comes with a default **`.gitignore`** file, but verify that it excludes sensitive and unnecessary files like cached data, logs, and environmental configuration.

To do this, create a **`.gitignore`** file in your project root and ensure it contains entries similar to the following:

```
/vendor
/node_modules
/public/storage
/storage/*.key
.env
```

These entries help maintain a clean repository by avoiding large binaries and sensitive credentials.

Adding Files to Repository

Now, add the project files to the repository using:

```
git add .
```

This command stages all current files in your directory for the first commit. After staging, make your initial commit with a clear, descriptive message:

```
git commit -m "Initial commit: Laravel 11 project setup with base configuration"
```

The clear commit messages are essential for maintaining a clean history and allowing your teammates to understand the purpose of each change.

Establishing Branch Conventions

To ensure a clean workflow, consider using branch naming conventions. For example, you might have branches named **`feature/*`**, **`bugfix/*`**, or **`release/*`** to categorize your work. Although setting up branches might not be part of this immediate step, thinking ahead and agreeing on commit and branch conventions within your team is of much help.

Configuring Remote Repositories

To do this, just link your local repository to the remote server by executing the following command. In the below, try to replace **<REMOTE_URL>** with the actual URL of your repository:

```
git remote add origin <REMOTE_URL>
```

This command associates your local Git repository with the remote repository to push your commits and collaborate with others. After adding the remote, push your commit to the remote repository by running:

```
git push -u origin master
```

This command pushes your local commits to the master branch of the remote repository and sets up tracking between your local and remote branches.

Ongoing Version Control Practices

As you work on your Laravel project, it's useful to frequently check the status of your repository:

```
git status
```

This command will help you track changes, identify untracked files, and confirm which files are staged for commit. Now you also need to remember to continue to commit regularly as you make changes.

For example, when adding new features or fixing bugs, use descriptive commit messages such as:

```
git commit -am "Feature: Add user authentication with Laravel
Passport"
```

The use of **`-am`** flag allows you to add all modified tracked files and commit them in one go in order to streamline the workflow.

Also, you must remember to synchronize your work with your teammates by pulling the latest changes before starting new work. It ensures that your local codebase is up to date with any changes made by your colleagues, reducing merge conflicts.

```
git pull origin master
```

This whole structured Git setup reinforces the comprehensive environment we're steadily establishing for your Laravel development, and also for future enhancements and team contributions.

Summary

At this point, you've got a solid foundation for developing Laravel on your Linux environment. You installed PHP 8.0 and the essential extensions, set up Composer to manage PHP dependencies, and used it to install Laravel 11 without a hitch. You configured your environment variables, generated the necessary application key, and verified your setup by running the Laravel development server. Then, you learned how to navigate Laravel's directory structure and set the right Linux file permissions for key folders like storage and bootstrap/cache. This made sure everything worked right and was secure. You also set up a solid development environment by installing key tools like PhpStorm, Laravel Debugbar, and Telescope, which upped your coding, debugging, and system monitoring skills. At last, you got Git version control set up for your project, came up with some commit conventions, and hooked your local repository up to remote platforms. That way, your team can work together and keep track of your code more easily. Every step builds on the previous one, getting you ready for more advanced projects without repeating what's already been done.

CHAPTER 2: ADVANCED ROUTING, CONTROLLERS, AND BLADE VIEWS

Overview

In this chapter, we're going to dive right into some advanced routing techniques, controller logic, and view rendering using Laravel. We will learn how to create dynamic routes that respond to user inputs, and then map them seamlessly to controller methods that can handle different data requests. We will also set up a resource controller to streamline CRUD operations, reduce code redundancy, and improve workflow efficiency.

Further, we will dive into Blade templating to pass and render complex, nested dynamic data in your views, making your frontend interactions more adaptive. And then, we will set up API-specific routes and write custom JSON responses to make sure your app can easily share data with outside clients. This chapter is going to help you build flexible, interactive, and robust applications, setting a strong foundation for tackling even more complex challenges later on in your Laravel development journey.

Recipe 1: Creating Dynamic Routes and Controller Logic

As you work on your Laravel application "myapp," you notice that as the project grows, static routes aren't enough to handle all the different user requests. So now you have decided that dynamic routing is essential. This approach lets your application interpret and process parameters in the URL, directing requests to the right controllers. So here in this recipe, we will learn how to define dynamic routes in your Laravel project, create the controller logic to match, and integrate a Blade view to render the output. It builds on your previous setup to make sure your application responds intelligently to different inputs.

Setting up a Dynamic Route

To begin with, we first navigate to the project directory "myapp", and then we open the **routes/web.php** file in our code editor. In this, we need. To add a new route that captures a dynamic segment from the URL using the following code:

```
Route::get('/user/{id}',
[App\Http\Controllers\UserController::class, 'show'])-
>name('user.show');
```

Here, the **{id}** part of the URL is dynamic, meaning that it can accept any value that represents a user identifier. This configuration directs all GET requests matching **/user/{id}** to the **show** method within the **UserController**.

Generating and Editing Controller

Creating UserController

We can generate the controller by running the following Artisan command:

```
php artisan make:controller UserController
```

This command creates a new file named **UserController.php** in the **app/Http/Controllers** directory.

Defining Controller Logic

To define the controller logic, we first open **UserController.php** and define the **show** method to handle the dynamic route. We update the controller as shown below:

```
<?php
namespace App\Http\Controllers;
use Illuminate\Http\Request;
class UserController extends Controller
{
    /**
     * Display the specified user.
     *
     * @param  int  $id
     * @return \Illuminate\View\View
     */
    public function show($id)
    {
        // For demonstration, we create a mock user array
        $user = [
            'id'    => $id,
            'name'  => 'User ' . $id,
            'email' => 'user' . $id . '@example.com'
        ];
        return view('user.show', compact('user'));
```

```
    }
}
```

This method retrieves (or simulates) user data based on the dynamic URL parameter, then passes the data to a view for rendering.

Creating Blade View to Render Data

For this, first navigate to the **resources/views** directory and create a new folder named **user**. Within this folder, create a file called **show.blade.php**. After this, insert the following HTML and Blade code into **show.blade.php**:

```
<!DOCTYPE html>
<html lang="en">
<head>
    <meta charset="UTF-8">
    <title>User Profile</title>
</head>
<body>
    <h1>User Profile for {{ $user['name'] }}</h1>
    <p>User ID: {{ $user['id'] }}</p>
    <p>Email: {{ $user['email'] }}</p>
</body>
</html>
```

This template uses Blade syntax to dynamically display the user info that's passed from the controller. By following these steps, you set up a dynamic routing system that connects URL parameters to your controller logic and shows the results using a Blade view.

Recipe 2: Using Resource Controllers for Efficient CRUD Operations

Let's say your "myapp" has gotten pretty complex, and you are having a hard time doing CRUD operations in a disorganized and inefficient way. During a team meeting, you all realize that managing CRUD functionalities individually for different models can lead to repetitive code and unorganized logic. We are going to use resource controllers to deal with this issue. It's a built-in

Laravel feature that handles CRUD operations by organizing the related methods in a single controller. This method will keep your code base clean, make it faster to develop, and easier to maintain as you build out your application.

Creating Resource Controller

To start with, we first generate a resource controller for a model in your application. Suppose you want to manage a "Product" model, so here, you run the following Artisan command in oyur project directory:

```
php artisan make:controller ProductController --resource
```

The above command creates a new file named **ProductController.php** in the **app/Http/Controllers** directory, which automatically comes with methods corresponding to the typical CRUD operations.

Understanding Resource Controller Methods

Within the newly created **ProductController.php**, you will observe methods such as:

- **index()**: Lists all the products.
- **create()**: Displays the form to create a new product.
- **store()**: Processes the form data to add a new product.
- **show($id)**: Displays a single product by its unique identifier.
- **edit($id)**: Displays the form to edit an existing product.
- **update($id)**: Processes the updated information for an existing product.
- **destroy($id)**: Deletes a product.

Each of the above method is designed to handle a specific part of the CRUD operations.

Defining Resource Routes

Now, to ensure that each of these controller methods is reachable, you need to define a resource route in your **routes/web.php** file as below:

```
Route::resource('products',
App\Http\Controllers\ProductController::class);
```

This single line automatically maps the standard HTTP verbs (GET, POST, PUT/PATCH, DELETE) to their corresponding methods in the **ProductController**. This efficient mapping simplifies routing and ensures consistent endpoint naming conventions across your application.

Recipe 3: Rendering Blade Templates with Dynamic Data

We are now up against a challenge where just rendering static content isn't enough. The more you use your Laravel application, the more complex and dynamic the information displayed will need to be, based on user interactions and backend data. At one of your team's project meetings recently, you shared about how important it is to be able to show all the info about the product, like images, features, and prices, in a way that's easy to see and understand. Today, we're going to learn how to use Blade templates, which is Laravel's powerful templating engine.We will see how to pass and render intricate data structures from your controllers to your views.

Blade Templates Overview

Blade is Laravel's intuitive templating engine that allows you to write clean, expressive syntax for your HTML. It streamlines rendering dynamic content using directives for control structures, loops, and data binding. Blade templates are stored in the **`resources/views`** directory and typically use the **`.blade.php`** extension. This setup means that you can easily switch between static HTML and dynamic content, combining PHP and HTML seamlessly. You will soon see how we can harness these capabilities to render complex data models passed from our controllers.

Passing Complex Data from Controller

Let us consider that we need to display a list of products with detailed information about each item. So for this, in your controller, you prepare a complex array or collection of product data. Open your ProductController and update a method to pass this structured data to a Blade view.

For example, you can modify a method named **`index()`** like this:

```
<?php
namespace App\Http\Controllers;
use Illuminate\Http\Request;
class ProductController extends Controller
{
    /**
     * Display a listing of the products.
     *
     * @return \Illuminate\View\View
     */
```

```
    public function index()
    {
        // Sample complex data: an array of products with
nested attributes.
        $products = [
            [
                'id' => 1,
                'name' => 'Smartphone Model X',
                'price' => 699.99,
                'features' => [
                    'Display' => '6.1 inch OLED',
                    'Battery' => '3700 mAh',
                    'Camera' => '12 MP dual rear camera'
                ],
                'images' => [
                    'front' => 'modelx-front.jpg',
                    'back' => 'modelx-back.jpg'
                ]
            ],
            [
                'id' => 2,
                'name' => 'Laptop Pro 15',
                'price' => 1299.99,
                'features' => [
                    'Display' => '15.6 inch Retina',
                    'Processor' => 'Intel i7',
                    'Memory' => '16 GB'
                ],
                'images' => [
                    'front' => 'laptoppro-front.jpg',
```

```
                    'side' => 'laptoppro-side.jpg'
                ]
            ]
        ];
        // Pass the data to the Blade view named
products.index
        return view('products.index', compact('products'));
    }
}
```

In the above, you create an array of products where each product has multiple nested attributes. This data structure can easily be expanded as you incorporate more detailed information from your database later on.

Creating Blade View to Render Dynamic Data

Now that the controller is passing complex data to the view, it's time to display this information dynamically using Blade syntax. To do this, let us first create a new Blade file at **resources/views/products/index.blade.php** and populate it with code that iterates over the products array and renders all necessary information:

```
<!DOCTYPE html>
<html lang="en">
<head>
    <meta charset="UTF-8">
    <title>Product Listings</title>
</head>
<body>
    <h1>Product Listings</h1>
    {{-- Loop through each product and display details --}}
    @foreach ($products as $product)
        <div style="border: 1px solid #ccc; padding: 15px;
margin-bottom: 15px;">
            <h2>{{ $product['name'] }} (ID: {{ $product['id']
}})</h2>
```

```
            <p>Price: ${{ number_format($product['price'], 2)
}}</p>
            <h3>Features:</h3>
            <ul>
                @foreach ($product['features'] as $key =>
$value)
                    <li><strong>{{ $key }}:</strong> {{ $value
}}</li>
                @endforeach
            </ul>
            <h3>Images:</h3>
            <ul>
                @foreach ($product['images'] as $view =>
$filename)
                    <li>{{ ucfirst($view) }} View: <img
src="/images/{{ $filename }}" alt="{{ $product['name'] }} {{
$view }}" width="100"></li>
                @endforeach
            </ul>
        </div>
    @endforeach
</body>
</html>
```

This view leverages Blade's **@foreach** loop to iterate over the **products** array, displaying each product's details in an organized format. It demonstrates how to handle nested arrays for features and images, allowing each key-value pair to be rendered neatly. The dynamic content rendered here adjusts according to the product data sent by the controller, ensuring that as your data complexity increases, your view will handle and display it appropriately. This integrated approach allows you to easily update the product information without manually modifying the HTML, as every change in the data source is automatically reflected in the rendered output.

Recipe 4: Designing API Routes and Custom

JSON Responses

While working on "myapp," you noticed that the standard web responses aren't meetng the needs of external clients or mobile applications. The current API responses don't have consistent formatting, which makes it hard for consumers to reliably parse data. During a team meeting, you realized that it's essential to organize API responses to make them clearer and easier to use. So today, we will learn how to define API-specific routes and craft custom JSON responses that provide a clean, predictable data format. This will make client-side processing more efficient and improve the reliability of your API endpoints.

Defining API-specific Routes

Firstly, open the **routes/api.php** file in "myapp". And then, instead of using web routes for API endpoints, you can keep API routes isolated for better management and middleware handling.

Then do add a new route that maps to a controller responsible for fetching product data as shown below:

```
Route::get('/products',
[App\Http\Controllers\Api\ProductApiController::class,
'index'])->name('api.products.index');
```

This route listens for GET requests to **/api/products** and directs them to the **index** method in the **ProductApiController** placed under the **App\Http\Controllers\Api** namespace.

Generating API Controller

Creating Controller

To create the controller, switch back to your terminal and generate the API controller using Artisan:

```
php artisan make:controller Api/ProductApiController
```

This command creates a new controller file in the **app/Http/Controllers/Api** directory. This separation keeps your API logic distinct from your web controllers, ensuring clean and focused code.

Adding Custom JSON Response Logic

Now here, open the newly created **ProductApiController.php** file and define the **index** method. Here, we will construct a JSON response that adheres to your desired structure as shown below:

```
<?php
namespace App\Http\Controllers\Api;
use App\Http\Controllers\Controller;
use Illuminate\Http\Request;
class ProductApiController extends Controller
{
    /**
     * Return a structured JSON response for products.
     *
     * @return \Illuminate\Http\JsonResponse
     */
    public function index()
    {
        // Prepare a sample list of products as an array of
associative arrays.
        $products = [
            [
                'id' => 1,
                'name' => 'Smartphone Model X',
                'price' => 699.99,
                'features' => [
                    'Display' => '6.1 inch OLED',
                    'Battery' => '3700 mAh',
                    'Camera' => '12 MP dual rear camera'
                ]
            ],
            [
```

```
                'id' => 2,
                'name' => 'Laptop Pro 15',
                'price' => 1299.99,
                'features' => [
                    'Display' => '15.6 inch Retina',
                    'Processor' => 'Intel i7',
                    'Memory' => '16 GB'
                ]
            ]
        ];
        // Define a custom response structure.
        $response = [
            'success' => true,
            'data'    => $products,
            'message' => 'Products fetched successfully.',
        ];
        // Return the JSON response with an appropriate HTTP
status code.
        return response()->json($response, 200);
    }
}
```

In the above code, the **`index`** method constructs a structured JSON response with three clear keys:

- **`success`**: A flag indicating the status of the request.
- **`data`**: The actual payload containing the list of products.
- **`message`**: A human-readable message providing additional context.

This structure ensures that any client consuming the API will receive consistent and predictable data.

Verifying Custom JSON Response

Now, to ensure your custom API endpoint works as expected, start your Laravel development server:

```
php artisan serve
```

Open a browser or an API testing tool like Postman, and navigate to:

```
http://127.0.0.1:8000/api/products
```

You should see a well-structured JSON response containing your sample products, the success flag, and a message. This confirms that your API routes and custom JSON responses are configured correctly.

Summary

In this chapter, you learned about the most important parts of Laravel's web architecture by exploring dynamic routing and strong controller logic. You started out by creating dynamic routes that captured URL segments and mapped them to controller methods, which helped the application process user requests efficiently. You made a new controller using Artisan and set up logic to handle these dynamic parameters, which made the process of accessing and processing data easier. Moving forward, you put in place a resource controller to streamline CRUD operations, cutting down on code duplication and making things easier to maintain.

Then you got into blade templating, learning how to pass complex, nested data from controllers to views for dynamic rendering of content. You also put together your API responses by setting up API-specific routes in the designated routes file, creating a dedicated API controller, and making custom JSON responses that made things clearer and more consistent for consumers. All these steps together made sure your application was easy to expand and maintain, and it met real-world needs well.

CHAPTER 3: AUTHENTICATION AND AUTHORIZATION PRACTICES

Overview

In this chapter, we will learn how to make your "myapp" more secure by improving how users are verified and authorized. We are going to learn how to integrate Laravel Breeze to establish a secure baseline for user login, registration, and password management. Also, we will use role-based access control with custom middleware to clearly define and enforce access hierarchies for different user roles.

We will also integrate social login functionality using Laravel Socialite to streamline user registration via popular social media platforms. To add an extra layer of security to your application, you are going to enable two-factor authentication with Laravel Fortify. This will protect user accounts. This chapter's gonna give you the lowdown on a bunch of security features that'll not only keep your app safe and sound, but also give you a flexible way to manage user permissions and access across your whole system.

Recipe 1: Building Secure User Authentication

There will be a time for your app where securing user access becomes essential. In a busy team meeting, you discussed the potential security risks and realized that implementing robust user authentication is key to protecting sensitive data and managing user sessions efficiently. Today, we have chosen to use Laravel Breeze—a lightweight starter kit for authentication—to ensure that user logins, registrations, and password management are handled securely. By integrating Breeze, you will simplify the process of managing user credentials and session security, making sure that every login attempt is processed correctly and that the overall authentication system remains both user-friendly and robust.

Installing Laravel Breeze

Laravel Breeze provides minimal, simple implementations of all of Laravel's authentication features using Blade templates. It offers all the essential routes, controllers, and views you need to support login, registration, password reset, and email verification out-of-the-box. Its streamlined design serves as an excellent starting point for those new to Laravel authentication while ensuring a secure environment.

So now, to implement secure user authentication, pull the Laravel Breeze as a development dependency by running:

```
composer require laravel/breeze --dev
```

Once the package is installed, initialize Breeze using the Artisan command:

```
php artisan breeze:install
```

This command scaffolds authentication routes, controllers, and views within your application.

Installing Frontend Dependencies

The Laravel Breeze's installation also sets up Tailwind CSS and other assets used in the authentication views. Install these dependencies by running:

```
npm install && npm run dev
```

This process compiles your assets, ensuring that your login and registration pages are both sleek and responsive.

Running Migrations and Testing Authentication

Before testing the authentication flows, run the database migrations to create the necessary tables for user management:

```
php artisan migrate
```

Once completed, start your development server:

```
php artisan serve
```

And finally, you need to visit your application and you should see ready-to-use login, registration, and password reset pages. All these pages ensure that credentials are processed securely and that sessions are managed correctly.

Recipe 2: Implementing RBAC

Since you are expanding your app to include sensitive areas that require controlled access based on user roles, it's important to keep security in mind. So, during a strategy session with your team, you decide that RBAC is vital to make sure that only authorized users can access certain endpoints. In our app, we're going to use roles like "admin", "editor", and "user" to control what each account can do. Today, we are going to use RBAC with Laravel middleware. We will learn how to set up middleware to check user roles, design permission hierarchies, and protect endpoints from unauthorized access. This'll help your app stay secure and follow business rules.

Creating Custom Middleware

First, we begin by creating a custom middleware that will verify a user's role by running:

```
php artisan make:middleware RoleMiddleware
```

This command creates a new file called **RoleMiddleware.php** in the **app/Http/Middleware** directory.

Then, we open the **RoleMiddleware.php** and update it to check the authenticated user's role. For example, suppose you want only users with an "admin" role to access specific routes. So, we modify the middleware as follows:

```
<?php
namespace App\Http\Middleware;
use Closure;
use Illuminate\Http\Request;
use Illuminate\Support\Facades\Auth;
class RoleMiddleware
{
    /**
     * Handle an incoming request.
     *
     * @param  \Illuminate\Http\Request  $request
     * @param  \Closure  $next
     * @param  string  $role
     * @return mixed
     */
    public function handle(Request $request, Closure $next,
$role)
    {
        if (!Auth::check()) {
            return redirect('/login');
        }
        // Check if the authenticated user has the required
role
        $user = Auth::user();
        if ($user->role !== $role) {
```

```
                abort(403, 'Unauthorized action.');
            }
            return $next($request);
        }
}
```

Here, the middleware ensures that only users whose **role** attribute matches the specified role can proceed. You can expand this logic to accept multiple roles if needed, by checking if the user's role exists in an array of permitted roles.

Registering Middleware

Now, to make the middleware available throughout your application, register it in the **app/Http/Kernel.php** file. In the **$routeMiddleware** array, we simply add an entry for your role middleware:

```
protected $routeMiddleware = [
    // other middleware entries
    'role' => \App\Http\Middleware\RoleMiddleware::class,
];
```

This step assigns the alias **role** to your middleware, making it easy to apply to routes.

Applying Middleware to Routes

Next, we update your routes to enforce role-based access control. For example, if you want to restrict access to admin-specific pages, we open the **routes/web.php** file and apply the middleware to a group of routes:

```
Route::group(['middleware' => ['auth', 'role:admin']],
function () {
    Route::get('/admin/dashboard',
[App\Http\Controllers\AdminController::class, 'dashboard'])-
>name('admin.dashboard');
    // Add more admin routes here
});
```

This grouping ensures that only authenticated users with an "admin" role can access the routes defined inside the group. Now here, you can create similar groups for other roles, such as editors.

Designing Permission Hierarchies

There will be situations and challenges in future where you might need more granular permissions. So here, instead of a single role check, you may simply consider expanding your middleware to verify if a user has one of several authorized roles.

To do this, we modify the middleware's handle method to accept multiple roles:

```
public function handle(Request $request, Closure $next,
...$roles)
{
    if (!Auth::check()) {
        return redirect('/login');
    }
    $user = Auth::user();
    if (!in_array($user->role, $roles)) {
        abort(403, 'Unauthorized action.');
    }
    return $next($request);
}
```

Then, apply it in your routes like so:

```
Route::group(['middleware' => ['auth', 'role:admin,editor']],
function () {
    Route::get('/management',
[App\Http\Controllers\ManagementController::class, 'index'])-
>name('management.index');
});
```

This structure lets you define a hierarchy of permissions, ensuring that both admins and editors can access the management section.

Recipe 3: Integrating Social Logins

Now after talking to other app developers and gauging the customer feedback, you realize that traditional authentication isn't sufficient for your growing user base. Your team discussed offering social media login options to simplify the registration process and attract a broader audience. You decided to leverage Laravel Socialite—a popular package that streamlines authentication with various social platforms—so that your users can log in using services like GitHub, Google, or Facebook. So here, we will integrate Socialite into your Linux-based Laravel environment. This will involve installing the package, configuring it with a GitHub, and setting up the necessary routes and controller methods to handle social login and callbacks.

Installing Laravel Socialite

Laravel Socialite is a first-class package that abstracts the complexities of OAuth authentication, allowing you to authenticate users via third-party providers seamlessly. It provides a simple interface to integrate multiple social providers, ensuring that your application maintains consistency and security across different login methods.

So now, to install this, we run the following command:

```
composer require laravel/socialite
```

We then confirm that Socialite is available in your application. The Laravel automatically registers Socialite via package auto-discovery, so no extra provider configuration is required in the **`config/app.php`** file.

Configuring Socialite for a Provider

For this demonstration, you will integrate GitHub social login for which you open the **`config/services.php`** file and add the GitHub configuration settings. You may also need to obtain the client ID, client secret, and callback URL from your GitHub OAuth app registration by doing the following:

```
'github' => [
    'client_id' => env('GITHUB_CLIENT_ID'),
    'client_secret' => env('GITHUB_CLIENT_SECRET'),
    'redirect' => env('GITHUB_REDIRECT_URI'),
],
```

Next, update your **`.env`** file with these credentials:

```
GITHUB_CLIENT_ID=your_github_client_id
GITHUB_CLIENT_SECRET=your_github_client_secret
GITHUB_REDIRECT_URI=http://127.0.0.1:8000/auth/github/callback
```

Setup Social Login Routes and Controller

You now need to create a controller to manage social authentication. For this, first generate a controller called **SocialAuthController** by running:

```
php artisan make:controller SocialAuthController
```

Next, open the newly created controller file and add two methods: one to redirect the user to GitHub's authentication page, and one to handle the callback as below:

```
<?php
namespace App\Http\Controllers;
use Laravel\Socialite\Facades\Socialite;
use Illuminate\Http\Request;
class SocialAuthController extends Controller
{
    // Redirect the user to the GitHub authentication page.
    public function redirectToProvider()
    {
        return Socialite::driver('github')->redirect();
    }
    // Obtain the user information from GitHub.
    public function handleProviderCallback()
    {
        $githubUser = Socialite::driver('github')->user();
        // You can now use $githubUser->token, $githubUser-
>getName(), etc.
        // Implement your logic to find or create a local user
record here.
        // For demonstration, simply return the user data.
        return response()->json($githubUser);
    }
}
```

Next, update your **routes/web.php** file to include routes for these methods:

```
Route::get('/auth/github',
[App\Http\Controllers\SocialAuthController::class,
'redirectToProvider'])->name('auth.github');
Route::get('/auth/github/callback',
[App\Http\Controllers\SocialAuthController::class,
'handleProviderCallback'])->name('auth.github.callback');
```

This whole setup will empower your application to offer secure and seamless login experiences through social platforms.

Recipe 4: Enforcing Two-Factor Authentication

You've already got secure user authentication, social logins, and role-based access control set up in the previous solution. And, now you want to add an extra layer of security with two-factor authentication (2FA). You and your team mentioned during the review meeting that 2FA is key to keeping accounts safe from unauthorized access. To meet this need, you decide to implement 2FA using Laravel Fortify, which integrates seamlessly with your existing authentication systems. We're going to walk through setting up Fortify for two-factor authentication, setting up the database columns you need, and testing the 2FA process in your Linux environment. And this feature makes it so that every login not only checks that we are who you say you are, but also asks you to do one more step to make your app even more secure.

Installing Laravel Fortify

In your "myapp" project directory, run the following command to install Laravel Fortify via Composer:

```
composer require laravel/fortify
```

The Fortify serves as the backend authentication implementation, providing support for two-factor authentication along with other enhanced security features. Once Fortify is installed, you can publish its configuration file by running:

```
php artisan vendor:publish --
provider="Laravel\Fortify\FortifyServiceProvider"
```

This above command creates a **config/fortify.php** file where you can manage the two-factor authentication settings.

Configuring Two-Factor Authentication

Here, we want to store the two-factor authentication credentials, for which you have to ensure the users table includes the necessary columns, which you can do by opening the migration file (or create a new one), in which you add fields like **two_factor_secret** and **two_factor_recovery_codes**.

Given below is a quick sample:

```
Schema::table('users', function (Blueprint $table) {
    $table->text('two_factor_secret')->nullable();
    $table->text('two_factor_recovery_codes')->nullable();
});
```

Then, run the migration to update your database:

```
php artisan migrate
```

After that, modify your user model to use the **TwoFactorAuthenticatable** trait provided by Fortify. This can be done by opening the **app/Models/User.php** and adding the following:

```
use Laravel\Fortify\TwoFactorAuthenticatable;
class User extends Authenticatable
{
    use TwoFactorAuthenticatable;
    // ...
}
```

Testing Two-Factor Authentication

Within the **config/fortify.php** file, we have to confirm that the two-factor authentication options are enabled. This can bedone by verifying that the **features** array includes two-factor authentication as below:

```
'features' => [
    // other features...
    Features::twoFactorAuthentication([
        'confirmPassword' => true,
    ]),
```

```
],
```

This setting ensures users must confirm their password when enabling or disabling 2FA. If you are using Laravel Breeze or another frontend scaffolding that integrates with Fortify, the two-factor authentication views will be available automatically. Otherwise, you may need to create your views or refer to Fortify's documentation for customizing the two-factor user interface.

After all this, then you need to start your development server:

```
php artisan serve
```

Then do as usual like login to your application, navigate to your user profile settings, and locate the two-factor authentication options. You can simply follow the on-screen instructions to enable 2FA, which typically includes generating a QR code that you scan with an authenticator app (such as Google Authenticator) on your mobile device. Your application will also generate recovery codes that you should store securely.

All these steps get you the integrated two-factor authentication into your app.

Summary

Throughout this chapter, you've been working on making your app more secure by setting up a solid authentication and authorization system. You started by integrating Laravel Breeze to set up a secure user authentication flow, which included configuring login, registration, and password reset functionalities using pre-built views and controllers. Then, you moved on to implementing RBAC by creating custom middleware that verified user roles, making sure that sensitive routes were accessible only to authorized users.

Next, you added more authentication features by using Laravel Socialite to integrate social logins, so users could sign in with their preferred social media accounts. You finally decided to step up security by setting up two-factor authentication using Laravel Fortify. This meant adding the necessary columns to the users table, updating the user model with the right trait, and changing Fortify's configuration to enable 2FA features. It's a pretty straightforward process: you get the user credentials, make sure the sessions are secure, and set up a solid access control system. All of this together boosts the security of your application.

Chapter 4: Database Models, Migrations, and Query Optimization

Overview

The goal of this chapter is to help you design, set up, and improve your database layer so that it can adapt to the changing needs of "myapp." We are going to learn how to make strong Eloquent models that handle one-to-many and many-to-many relationships, so you can easily get your data and manage it. We will work on creating and executing migration files using Laravel Artisan on your Linux setup, making sure that your database schema evolves alongside your application. We will also learn about data seeding techniques to generate consistent, realistic test datasets for thorough development and quality assurance.

The chapter will also teach you some advanced ways to optimize your queries, like using eager loading to cut down on redundant database calls and boost performance. As you go through this, we will be building on practical examples and verified tools like Laravel Debugbar. This'll help you take a cohesive and scalable approach to managing your application's data layer.

Recipe 1: Defining Database Models and Relationships

Now that you've made some progress with your app, it's time to start modeling the relationships in your database the right way. Your application is evolving, and you need to define how data entities interact. For example, you want each user to be able to write multiple posts (a one-to-many relationship) while each post can be associated with several tags, and each tag can belong to multiple posts (a many-to-many relationship). At a meeting we had recently, your team decided that organizing these relationships would make managing data and running queries easier. Now, we will learn how to build Eloquent models that handle both one-to-many and many-to-many relationships. This way, your app can handle data interactions smoothly and efficiently.

Creating Post and Tag Models

To begin with, we first generate the models along with migration files. For this, simply run:

```
php artisan make:model Post -m
php artisan make:model Tag -m
```

This command creates the Post and Tag models along with their associated migration files.

Defining One-to-Many Relationship

Since Laravel provides a built-in User model, we will enhance it by establishing that each user can have multiple posts. We will open the User model file (**`app/Models/User.php`**) and add the following method:

```
public function posts()
{
    return $this->hasMany(Post::class);
}
```

Next, update the Post model (**app/Models/Post.php**) to reflect the inverse relationship. In Post, add:

```
public function user()
{
    return $this->belongsTo(User::class);
}
```

Now here, you need to ensure that the Post model is ready to accept necessary fields by defining fillable properties:

```
protected $fillable = ['title', 'content', 'user_id'];
```

Defining Many-to-Many Relationship

In your Post model, add a method for the many-to-many association with tags:

```
public function tags()
{
    return $this->belongsToMany(Tag::class);
}
```

Then, in the Tag model (**app/Models/Tag.php**), define the reciprocal method:

```
public function posts()
{
    return $this->belongsToMany(Post::class);
}
```

Creating Pivot Table Migration

To support the many-to-many relationship, we need to generate a migration for the pivot table:

```
php artisan make:migration create_post_tag_table --
create=post_tag
```

Next, open the newly created migration file (in the **database/migrations** directory) and set up the pivot table schema:

```
public function up()
{
    Schema::create('post_tag', function (Blueprint $table) {
        $table->id();
        $table->foreignId('post_id')->constrained()-
>onDelete('cascade');
        $table->foreignId('tag_id')->constrained()-
>onDelete('cascade');
        $table->timestamps();
    });
}
public function down()
{
    Schema::dropIfExists('post_tag');
}
```

Finally, we need to run the migration to create the necessary tables:

```
php artisan migrate
```

With all these simply steps, you can structure your models to reflect both one-to-many and many-to-many relationships. This confirms that your app handles user-post and post-tag interactions efficiently.

Recipe 2: Creating and Executing Migrations

Next, we need to learn to lock down your database design with migrations. This is a key part of your Laravel development workflow. In team chat recently, you said that having migration files ready makes it so your whole team can version control and sync database schema changes without a hitch. Here's how to generate those migration files using Artisan commands and run them on your Linux system.

Generating Migration Files

If you want to generate a migration for, let's say, a new "Comments" table, here's the Artisan command we will need to use:

```
php artisan make:migration create_comments_table --
create=comments
```

This command creates a migration file in the **database/migrations** folder. The file name begins with a timestamp, which helps maintain the order of migrations.

Customizing Migration File

Next, open the newly generated migration file in our IDE. You will see a structure with **up()** and **down()** methods. In the **up()** method, define the schema for the “comments” table as shown in the following example:

```
public function up()
{
    Schema::create('comments', function (Blueprint $table) {
        $table->id();
        $table->foreignId('post_id')->constrained()-
>onDelete('cascade');
        $table->string('author');
        $table->text('content');
        $table->timestamps();
    });
}
```

This above script sets up a “comments” table with a primary key, a foreign key linking to a post, author information, content, and timestamps.

Executing Migrations

Once you’ve customized your migration file, it’s time to apply the changes to your database as shown below:

```
php artisan migrate
```

This command executes all outstanding migrations, creating the tables and fields as defined. If you need to check the current status of migrations, you may use:

```
php artisan migrate:status
```

This command will display which migrations have been run, confirming that your database schema is up to date.

Recipe 3: Data Seeding for Consistent Testing Scenarios

Now somehow, you may come to a realization that having a consistent and realistic dataset is of much help for testing new features and ensuring that your application behaves as expected. So, during a code review session, your team agreed that simulating real-world data would help identify potential issues early in the development cycle. With this in mind, you decided to use Laravel's seeding functionality to populate your database with test data. So, let us now learn to write seed classes, execute them using Artisan commands, and verify that your database is populated with the required sample data, providing a reliable testing environment.

Creating a Seeder Class

Firstr, run the following to create a new seeder for a relevant model, such as posts:

```
php artisan make:seeder PostsTableSeeder
```

This command creates a new seeder file named **PostsTableSeeder.php** in the **database/seeders** directory.

Writing Seeder Logic

Next, open the newly created file (**database/seeders/PostsTableSeeder.php**) and update the **run()** method to insert realistic test data. You might insert data manually or use a factory for dynamic data generation. For example:

```
<?php
namespace Database\Seeders;
use Illuminate\Database\Seeder;
use Illuminate\Support\Facades\DB;
```

```
use Carbon\Carbon;
class PostsTableSeeder extends Seeder
{
    public function run()
    {
        // Insert sample posts into the 'posts' table
        DB::table('posts')->insert([
            [
                'title' => 'First Post',
                'content' => 'This is the content of the first
post.',
                'user_id' => 1,
                'created_at' => Carbon::now(),
                'updated_at' => Carbon::now()
            ],
            [
                'title' => 'Second Post',
                'content' => 'Here is some content for the
second post.',
                'user_id' => 1,
                'created_at' => Carbon::now(),
                'updated_at' => Carbon::now()
            ]
        ]);
    }
}
```

Alternatively, if you have defined model factories, you could call them here for generating multiple records dynamically.

Registering and Executing Seeders

Next, open the **DatabaseSeeder.php** file located in **database/seeders** and register the new seeder by adding the call within the **run()** method:

```
public function run()
{
    $this->call([
        PostsTableSeeder::class,
    ]);
}
```

Then, get the following command to run all seeders:

```
php artisan db:seed
```

This command populates your database with the test data defined in your seeder classes. You can verify that the data has been inserted correctly by connecting to your database using a tool like MySQL client, phpMyAdmin, or any database GUI, and checking the contents of the **posts** table.

Recipe 4: Optimizing Complex Database Queries

It looks like your app is having some performance issues when it comes to retrieving posts and comments. You figured out that the N+1 query problem was behind the slowdown. This issue comes up when you fetch all the posts and then loop through each one to get its comments, which makes an extra query for every post. To solve this in our Laravel 11 project running on Linux,we will use Laravel's built-in eager loading feature. Now, we will learn how to improve your data retrieval by using eager loading, a specific method provided by Laravel's Eloquent ORM. This is a pretty precise and effective approach. It makes sure that all the necessary data is fetched in a minimal number of queries, which consistently boosts performance across your application.We will also check the performance improvement using Laravel Debugbar, a tool we installed earlier in our environment via Composer, and confirmed through PhpStorm.We will be using our standard Linux development setup in "myapp" to execute all the steps.

Identify N+1 Query Problem

Here's some code you might want to consider. It'll get all the posts and then loop over each to access the comments:

```
$posts = App\Models\Post::all();
foreach ($posts as $post) {
    $comments = $post->comments; // Each iteration fires an
extra query
}
```

This results in one query to fetch posts plus one additional query per post to retrieve its comments, which can overwhelm the system as the number of posts increases.

Implement Eager Loading

To optimize this, we need to update your query to use Laravel's eager loading feature. In your controller method (for example, in PostController):

```
$posts = App\Models\Post::with('comments')->get();
```

This single modification instructs Laravel to fetch all posts and load all associated comments in just two queries—one for posts and one for the comments.

Verify Performance

Since we have Laravel Debugbar already installed in your app via Composer, you may simply run your application using:

```
php artisan serve
```

Then navigate to the page where posts and comments are displayed. With Laravel Debugbar active, observe the number of queries executed. You should see that instead of multiple queries for each post, only two queries are executed regardless of the number of posts.

Summary

During this chapter, you made some great strides in the data layer of your app. You established solid database models and mechanisms to efficiently handle schema changes and optimize queries. You started out by creating Eloquent models that defined one-to-many relationships (like users having multiple posts) and many-to-many relationships (such as posts tagged with multiple tags). You used Artisan to generate migration files, added the necessary fields and relationships, and then executed the migrations on your Linux system. Then, you enhanced the development and testing environment by writing and running seed classes to populate your database with realistic test data. You finally took care of those performance issues by tweaking those tricky database queries with eager loading. That really cut down on the number of queries and sped things up. All the steps were built on solid principles, so you could be sure that your database interactions were both scalable and maintainable.

CHAPTER 5: ROBUST DATA VALIDATION AND ERROR MANAGEMENT

Overview

We'll cover how to build a solid foundation for data validation and error management in this chapter. We are going to set up a solid server-side validation system that strictly enforces business rules using Laravel's Validator, making sure that every input meets the required standards. We will learn advanced techniques for creating custom validation rules and generating user-friendly error messages that are tailored to your app's specific needs.

In addition, we are going to make handling exceptions easier by setting up the Handler class to catch and log all errors in the same way. This will keep things running smoothly for users, even when problems pop up. We will also integrate a real-time monitoring solution using Laravel Pulse, which will track and display application errors continuously. This all-in-one approach will help your team figure out, fix, and fix any problems quickly, making your app more stable and performing better overall.

Recipe 1: Implementing Server-Side Data Validation

It's great to see you enhancing your app to manage user data reliably. Let us consider the situation wherein your team in recent review meet, discovered that inconsistencies and potential security vulnerabilities could arise without proper validation of user inputs. To make sure your data follows the rules and is formatted correctly, you decided to use strong server-side validation. In our Linux-based Laravel 11 environment managed via PhpStorm and using Laravel Breeze for authentication, it's super important to enforce data validation. Now, we will learn to use Laravel's built-in Validator to enforce server-side data validation rules. This ensures that every incoming request is processed correctly and follows your business logic.

Introducing Laravel's Validator

In practice, data validation is the first line of defense against invalid or malicious inputs. Business rules say that certain fields—like email addresses, passwords, and usernames—have to follow certain formats and rules. For example, you can make sure that user emails are unique and formatted properly, that passwords are at least a certain length, and that names consist only of alphabetic characters.

Laravel's got a solid validation engine that's both powerful and elegant. The Validator makes it simple to enforce rules on any incoming request. With a syntax that is both expressive and flexible, you can specify multiple validation rules for your data in one place. Laravel's validation system gives you clear error messages so you and your users know what needs to be corrected.

Implementing Server-Side Data Validation

We consider that we have a controller handling a user registration request. We open the controller file (for example, **RegisterController.php**) and modify the registration method as follows:

```
public function register(Request $request)
{
    // Define the validation rules based on business
requirements
    $rules = [
        'name'     => 'required|string|max:255|regex:/^[a-zA-
Z\s]+$/',
        'email'    => 'required|email|max:255|unique:users',
        'password' => 'required|string|min:8|confirmed',
    ];
    // Perform validation using Laravel's Validator
    $validatedData = $request->validate($rules);
    // If validation passes, create the new user
    // User::create([...]);
    // Return a response or redirect as needed
    return response()->json(['message' => 'User registered
successfully.']);
}
```

Based on the above script, the **validate()** method automatically checks the incoming request data against the defined rules.

- The **name** field is required, must be a string, and can only contain alphabetic characters and spaces.
- The **email** must be correctly formatted, unique in the users table, and within the proper length.
- The **password** requires confirmation and must meet a minimum length.

If any of these rules fail, Laravel will automatically return a response with error messages, prompting the user to make the necessary corrections.

Recipe 2: Custom Validation Rules & Feedback

With maturity reaching your app, you may recognize that the built-in validation rules sometimes do not cover all of your business needs. So, in your development meeting, you noted that certain inputs require specialized checks beyond what Laravel's default validators provide. For example, you may need to validate that a username doesn't contain prohibited words or that a discount code follows a custom pattern. Your goal is to provide precise, helpful error messages so that end users know exactly what to correct when their inputs do not meet your unique criteria. Here, you will craft custom validation rules in your app and implement tailored feedback to guide users clearly.

Writing Custom Validation Logic

Let's say you need to make sure a username doesn't have any banned terms. In your controller, go ahead and modify the validation rules by adding a closure for the custom validation logic. For example, in a registration method:

```
public function register(Request $request)
{
    $rules = [
        'username' => [
            'required',
            'string',
            'max:50',
            function ($attribute, $value, $fail) {
                $bannedWords = ['admin', 'root', 'superuser'];
                foreach ($bannedWords as $word) {
                    if (stripos($value, $word) !== false) {
                        return $fail("The $attribute cannot
contain the word '{$word}'.");
                    }
                }
            },
        ],
        'email'    => 'required|email|max:255|unique:users',
```

```
        'password' => 'required|string|min:8|confirmed',
    ];
    $validatedData = $request->validate($rules);
    // Proceed with creating the user once validation passes.
    // User::create([...]);
    return response()->json(['message' => 'User registered
successfully.']);
}
```

In the above, a closure is used to check if the **username** contains any banned words. If a match is found, the **$fail** callback triggers with a custom error message.

Developing Tailored Error Messages

While the Laravel automatically generates error messages for standard rules, custom validations allow you to provide targeted and clear feedback for users. In the custom validator defined above, we've given specific details like the prohibited word that was detected. To further enhance usability, you could also define custom error messages in a language file or directly within the validation call using the second parameter of the **validate()** method as shown in the following script:

```
$messages = [
    'username.required' => 'Please provide a username.',
    'username.max'      => 'Your username should not exceed 50
characters.',
    'email.required'    => 'An email address is required for
registration.',
    'email.email'       => 'Please enter a valid email
address.',
    'password.required' => 'A password is required.',
    'password.min'      => 'The password must be at least 8
characters long.',
    'password.confirmed' => 'The password confirmation does
not match.',
];
```

```
$validatedData = $request->validate($rules, $messages);
```

Now, you are ready to develop custom validation logic and tailored feedback that clearly communicates precise issues to your users. This will reinforce the security and integrity of the data in "myapp."

Recipe 3: Centralized Exception Handling

After a while, you figured out that unexpected errors and exceptions are bound to pop up when there's a ton of traffic and a lot of people are engaged. To deal with these issues head on, you decided to centralize exception handling by setting up Laravel's built-in exception framework. Today, we will learn how to use the Handler class to capture, log, and format errors consistently. This approach makes sure that every exception is managed in one place, making your application robust and easier to debug, while maintaining a user-friendly interface even when errors occur.We will be working in our usual Laravel environment on Linux, using PhpStorm and Laravel Debugbar to help us figure out any problems.

Customizing Report Method

Every Laravel project includes a central exception handler located at **app/Exceptions/Handler.php**. This file contains two primary methods: **report()** and **render()**. The **report()** method is responsible for logging the exception details, while **render()** is tasked with returning a suitable response to the user.

First, open the **app/Exceptions/Handler.php** in PhpStorm and you will see the default implementations provided by Laravel.

In the **report()** method, you can add custom logic to log additional details or integrate third-party error tracking services. For instance, you might decide to only log critical exceptions or format them in a specific structure. The default implementation already uses Laravel's logging facilities via the Log facade. You can adjust the logic as needed as shown in the following:

```
public function report(Throwable $exception)
{
    // Customize logging, or integrate with an error tracking
service like Sentry.
    if ($this->shouldReport($exception)) {
        \Log::error('Exception occurred: ' . $exception-
>getMessage(), [
            'exception' => $exception
```

```
        ]);
    }
    parent::report($exception);
}
```

Here, you check whether the exception should be reported and log the error message along with the exception details.

Customizing Render Method

The **render()** method converts exceptions into HTTP responses. You can tailor this method to handle different types of exceptions differently or to return custom JSON responses for API endpoints. Update the **render()** method as follows:

```
public function render($request, Throwable $exception)
{
    // Handle API exceptions: if the request expects JSON,
return a custom JSON response.
    if ($request->wantsJson()) {
        return response()->json([
            'success' => false,
            'message' => 'An error occurred.',
            'error'   => $exception->getMessage()
        ], 500);
    }
    // For web requests, return the default error view with
relevant status code.
    return parent::render($request, $exception);
}
```

This change ensures that when an API client sends a request (typically expecting a JSON response), the exception is rendered in a consistent format that includes a success flag, an error message, and the exception details. Otherwise, for standard web requests, Laravel's default error page is returned.

Testing Exception Handling

To test these configurations, you can manually throw an exception in one of your controller methods. For example, add the following line temporarily to simulate an error:

```
throw new \Exception('Testing centralized exception
handling.');
```

Then, visit the relevant route via your browser or API client. Use Laravel Debugbar to verify that the exception is logged and the response is properly formatted according to your settings in the **`render()`** method. This setup captures every unexpected error, logs it appropriately, and returns user-friendly responses based on the request type.

Recipe 4: Monitoring App Errors

Now consider that, after deploying your app, your team observed intermittent errors and performance issues that were difficult to diagnose using traditional logs alone. To enhance your troubleshooting workflow, you decided to integrate Laravel Pulse—a specialized package for real-time logging and monitoring. Laravel Pulse collects error logs, warnings, and system performance metrics and presents them on an interactive dashboard. This setup, running on your Linux-based Laravel environment managed via PhpStorm with Laravel Debugbar already installed, aims to provide immediate visibility into application health. For this, we will install Laravel Pulse, configure it for centralized logging, and see a practical monitoring scenario where a simulated error is captured and displayed on the Pulse dashboard to quickly track and resolve issues.

Installing Laravel Pulse

Laravel Pulse is designed to capture and display real-time logs and system events from your Laravel application. It integrates seamlessly with Laravel's built-in logging system, allowing you to focus on monitoring critical issues. Pulse aggregates error messages, warnings, and performance data, so you can see trends and anomalies over time. With this tool, we will have a single dashboard that provides an at-a-glance view of the application's health and a detailed log of events, making it easier to diagnose issues as they occur in production.

So now, to add Laravel Pulse to your "myapp", we need to run the similar Composer command as we did previously for all the other tools:

```
composer require laravel/pulse
```

The Laravel's package auto-discovery takes care of registering the Pulse service provider, so there's no need to manually edit your **`config/app.php`**. Once done, publish the configuration file and assets by running:

```
php artisan vendor:publish --
provider="Laravel\Pulse\PulseServiceProvider"
```

This command creates a configuration file at **config/pulse.php** and publishes the necessary frontend assets required for the Pulse dashboard. After this, try reviewing the configuration file to familiarize yourself with available options such as log levels, update frequencies, and dashboard styling.

Configuring Logging Channels

Now in order to confirm that the Pulse captures the right logs, we will configure a dedicated logging channel in your Laravel application. For this, we will first open the **config/logging.php** file and add a new channel named **pulse**:

```
'channels' => [
    // ... existing channels
    'pulse' => [
        'driver' => 'daily',
        'path' => storage_path('logs/pulse.log'),
        'level' => 'error',
        'days' => 14,
    ],
],
```

Then, update your **.env** file so that, at least in production or during testing, your application writes error logs to this channel:

```
LOG_CHANNEL=pulse
```

This configuration ensures that all critical issues and errors are directed to a dedicated log file that Laravel Pulse monitors continuously.

Integrating Laravel Pulse

The Laravel Pulse automatically picks up the standard logs generated by Laravel. In addition to automatic log capturing, you can log custom messages to the Pulse channel. For instance, in one of your controller actions, you might add:

```
use Illuminate\Support\Facades\Log;
```

```
public function processData()
{
    // Simulate a critical error condition
    try {
        // Some code that might fail
        throw new \Exception('Simulated critical failure in
processData.');
    } catch (\Exception $e) {
        Log::channel('pulse')->error('Critical error in
processData method', [
            'error'   => $e->getMessage(),
            'user_id' => auth()->id(),
            'action' => 'processData'
        ]);
    }
}
```

This explicit logging sends crucial error details to the Pulse log, and due to this, all these issues are visible in the monitoring dashboard.

For instance, if a critical error happens repeatedly, your Pulse dashboard will show a spike in error frequency. This visual indicator alerts you to a potential systemic issue that might require immediate attention, such as a bug in the data processing logic or a misconfiguration in a third-party API integration. In parallel, you can use Laravel Debugbar (which is already integrated into in our myapp) to cross-check the number of queries and performance metrics.

Customizing Alerts for Proactive Monitoring

To further enhance the monitoring setup, we can add a custom alert setting that sends notifications through email or Slack when an error of "critical" level is logged:

```
'alerts' => [
    'critical' => [
        'enabled'  => true,
        'channels' => ['mail', 'slack'],
        'mail'     => [
```

```
            'to'       => 'devteam@example.com',
            'subject' => 'Critical Error in myapp',
        ],
        'slack'    => [
            'webhook_url' => env('SLACK_WEBHOOK_URL'),
        ],
    ],
],
```

After setting this configuration, any log message designated as critical will trigger an alert. When the simulated error occurs during testing, your designated channels (such as email or Slack) will receive a notification, prompting your team to investigate immediately.

Once you have set up Laravel Pulse and customized alerts, it becomes a continuous process to monitor the Pulse dashboard. This system not only captures detailed logs and error events but also aggregates them on an intuitive dashboard, enabling your development team to swiftly track and resolve issues as they arise.

Summary

During this chapter, you made some great advances in how your app handles data integrity and error management. You started by using Laravel's Validator to make sure every request followed the business rules and data formats. You defined specific validation rules for important fields like username, email, and password, which helped keep data consistent and users secure. Then, you used closures to create custom validation logic, which let you enforce specialized constraints and give users customized error messages.

Later, you centralized exception handling by configuring Laravel's Handler class, which let you capture, log, and gracefully render unexpected errors. You also integrated a real-time monitoring solution by setting up Laravel Pulse, creating a dedicated logging channel, and testing the monitoring functionality through simulated errors. Each step in this chapter built on the last one, so the application validated inputs effectively and also had robust error logging and monitoring. These practices made the app more stable and gave your development team clear, actionable feedback to quickly resolve issues.

Chapter 6: Alerts, Notifications, and Performance Monitoring

Overview

In this chapter, we will learn to improve your app's responsiveness and user engagement by setting up a solid system for alerts, notifications, and performance monitoring. We are going to learn how to set up in-app alerts using Laravel's Notification system so that users get real-time feedback about critical events. We will also learn how to set up notifications for different channels, like email and text, so that your users get the important updates no matter where they are.

Later, we will integrate push notification capabilities using Laravel Broadcasting with Pusher and Laravel Echo, which will enable instant delivery of messages directly to users' browsers. And finally, we will use Laravel Telescope and Debugbar to keep an eye on key metrics like execution times, memory usage, and query efficiency. So, this chapter is all about giving you the know-how to keep your app running like a well-oiled machine and keep users happy by quickly fixing any hiccups.

Recipe 1: Deploying Real-time In-app Alerts

In "myapp," you figured out that sending out alerts in real-time is key to keeping users up-to-date with what's going on. In a recent team meeting, you found that users were missing important updates, like new messages, system warnings, or promotional notifications. It wasn't ideal to rely on external tools. You wanted to use Laravel's built-in features to create a seamless and efficient alert system within your application. Then, we will use Laravel's Notification system with database channels to set up in-app alerts. This approach lets you store notifications in the database and show them right in the app. We'll define and send notifications, store them in the database, and finally retrieve and display these alerts on the user interface.

Enabling Database Notifications in App

The Laravel's Notification system is built to handle multiple channels, including email, SMS, and the database. For in-app alerts, we will use the database channel. To do this, first open your **app/Models/User.php** file and confirm that the User model uses the **Notifiable** trait. This enables the user to receive notifications.

```
<?php
namespace App\Models;
use Illuminate\Foundation\Auth\User as Authenticatable;
use Illuminate\Notifications\Notifiable;
class User extends Authenticatable
{
```

```
    use Notifiable;
    // Model properties and methods...
}
```

The Laravel then automatically provides a migration for notifications if you use the built-in notification system. If it hasn't been published, then simply run the following:

```
php artisan notifications:table
php artisan migrate
```

This creates a **notifications** table in your database to store incoming notifications.

Creating Custom Notification In-App Alerts

We now create a custom notification that will be used as an in-app alert by running the following command:

```
php artisan make:notification UserAlertNotification
```

This command creates a new file at app/Notifications/UserAlertNotification.php. Now, to implement the notification, first open the generated notification file and update it to use the **toDatabase** method.

For in-app alerts, we want the notification's data stored in the database.

```
<?php
namespace App\Notifications;
use Illuminate\Bus\Queueable;
use Illuminate\Notifications\Notification;
use Illuminate\Contracts\Queue\ShouldQueue;
use Illuminate\Notifications\Messages\MailMessage;
class UserAlertNotification extends Notification
{
    use Queueable;
    protected $alertMessage;
    protected $alertType;
    /**
```

```
     * Create a new notification instance.
     *
     * @return void
     */
    public function __construct($alertMessage, $alertType =
'info')
    {
        $this->alertMessage = $alertMessage;
        $this->alertType = $alertType;
    }
    /**
     * Get the notification's delivery channels.
     *
     * @param  mixed  $notifiable
     * @return array
     */
    public function via($notifiable)
    {
        // We will use the 'database' channel for in-app
alerts.
        return ['database'];
    }
    /**
     * Get the array representation of the notification.
     *
     * @param  mixed  $notifiable
     * @return array
     */
    public function toDatabase($notifiable)
    {
```

```
        return [
            'message' => $this->alertMessage,
            'type'    => $this->alertType,
            'timestamp' => now()->toDateTimeString(),
        ];
    }
    // You could also define toMail() if you plan to support
email notifications in the future.
}
```

Here, the notification stores an alert message, a type (like 'info', 'warning', or 'error'), and a timestamp. These details will help you categorize and display the alerts in the UI.

Sending In-App Alerts

Now that you have your notification set up, the next step is to send it to users from your application. In one of your controller methods (for example, in a DashboardController), you can trigger an alert when a specific action occurs. For this, simply open the corresponding controller file and modify a method as follows:

```
<?php
namespace App\Http\Controllers;
use App\Models\User;
use App\Notifications\UserAlertNotification;
use Illuminate\Http\Request;
class DashboardController extends Controller
{
    public function show()
    {
        // Assume we are sending an in-app alert to the
currently authenticated user.
        $user = auth()->user();
        // Prepare a sample alert message and send the
notification.
```

```
        $alertMessage = 'You have a new system update
available!';
        $alertType = 'info';
        $user->notify(new UserAlertNotification($alertMessage,
$alertType));
        // Render the dashboard view (which will display
notifications).
        return view('dashboard');
    }
}
```

This above snippet sends an in-app alert to the authenticated user each time the Dashboard's show method is invoked.

Displaying In-App Alerts

The next step is to retrieve and display these notifications within your application. Typically, you might add a notifications dropdown or a dedicated section in your layout. In any Blade view (for example, your main layout file **resources/views/layouts/app.blade.php**), you can access the logged-in user's notifications using the **notifications** relationship provided by the Notifiable trait as below:

```
<!DOCTYPE html>
<html lang="en">
<head>
    <meta charset="UTF-8">
    <meta name="viewport" content="width=device-width,
initial-scale=1.0">
    <title>myapp</title>
    <!-- Include your CSS and JS assets here -->
</head>
<body>
    <nav>
        <!-- Navigation elements -->
        <div class="notifications">
```

```
            <h4>Notifications</h4>
            <ul>
                @foreach (auth()->user()->unreadNotifications as $notification)
                    <li class="alert alert-{{ $notification->data['type'] }}">
                        {{ $notification->data['message'] }}
                        <small>{{ $notification->data['timestamp'] }}</small>
                    </li>
                @endforeach
            </ul>
        </div>
    </nav>
    <div class="container">
        @yield('content')
    </div>
    <!-- Optionally include a script to mark notifications as read -->
    <script>
        // Example JavaScript for marking notifications as read via an AJAX call.
        // You may implement this if needed for a smoother user experience.
    </script>
</body>
</html>
```

In the above, we iterate over the current user's unread notifications and display them as alerts. Each notification shows the message, type (which can be styled with corresponding CSS classes), and the timestamp.

If youn want to further enhance usability, you might allow users to mark notifications as read as Laravel provides a method to mark all notifications as read:

```
<a href="{{ route('notifications.markAsRead') }}">Mark all as
read</a>
```

We then create a route and corresponding controller method to handle this:

```
// In routes/web.php
Route::get('/notifications/mark-as-read',
[App\Http\Controllers\NotificationController::class,
'markAsRead'])->name('notifications.markAsRead');
// In app/Http/Controllers/NotificationController.php
namespace App\Http\Controllers;
use Illuminate\Http\Request;
class NotificationController extends Controller
{
    public function markAsRead(Request $request)
    {
        auth()->user()->unreadNotifications->markAsRead();
        return redirect()->back();
    }
}
```

This allows users to clear their in-app alerts after reviewing them. This whole method ensures that any critical updates or system messages are delivered to users in real time and displayed in a user-friendly format.

Recipe 2: Configuring Email & SMS Notifications

Let us say that you realized that your users also need to be alerted to important events outside of the app. Your team discussed that email notifications and SMS alerts would be valuable for critical updates, such as account security warnings or transactional alerts, ensuring users stay informed wherever they are. So here, you will learn how to configure and send notifications through these channels using Laravel's native tools. We will create a notification class for important events, set up the necessary configurations in our Linux environment, and demonstrate how Laravel sends email messages and SMS alerts.

Creating Notification Class

We first start with the generation of a new notification class called **ImportantEventNotification** using the Artisan command as below:

```
php artisan make:notification ImportantEventNotification
```

This command creates a file at **app/Notifications/ImportantEventNotification.php**, which you will use to define how the notification is sent through different channels.

Implementing Email and SMS Notification Channels

You now open the previously generated file in PhpStorm and update the class so that it sends notifications via both email and SMS using Laravel's built-in channels as shown below:

```
<?php
namespace App\Notifications;
use Illuminate\Bus\Queueable;
use Illuminate\Notifications\Notification;
use Illuminate\Notifications\Messages\MailMessage;
use Illuminate\Notifications\Messages\NexmoMessage; // Use
VonageMessage if on Laravel 9+
class ImportantEventNotification extends Notification
{
    use Queueable;
    protected $eventMessage;
    protected $eventDetails;
    /**
     * Create a new notification instance.
     *
     * @param  string  $eventMessage
     * @param  array   $eventDetails
     * @return void
     */
```

```
    public function __construct($eventMessage, $eventDetails =
[])
    {
        $this->eventMessage = $eventMessage;
        $this->eventDetails = $eventDetails;
    }
    /**
     * Get the notification's delivery channels.
     *
     * @param  mixed  $notifiable
     * @return array
     */
    public function via($notifiable)
    {
        // We will use both mail and SMS channels.
        return ['mail', 'nexmo']; // If using Laravel 9,
replace 'nexmo' with 'vonage'
    }
    /**
     * Get the mail representation of the notification.
     *
     * @param  mixed  $notifiable
     * @return \Illuminate\Notifications\Messages\MailMessage
     */
    public function toMail($notifiable)
    {
        // Customize the email content as needed.
        return (new MailMessage)
                    ->subject('Important Update from myapp')
```

```
                    ->greeting('Hello ' . $notifiable->name .
',')
                    ->line($this->eventMessage)
                    ->line('Additional Details:')
                    ->line(implode(', ', $this->eventDetails))
                    ->action('View Details',
url('/dashboard'))
                    ->line('Thank you for using our
application!');
    }
    /**
     * Get the Nexmo / SMS representation of the notification.
     *
     * @param  mixed  $notifiable
     * @return \Illuminate\Notifications\Messages\NexmoMessage
     */
    public function toNexmo($notifiable)
    {
        // Compose a concise SMS message.
        return (new NexmoMessage)
                    ->content('Important update: ' . $this-
>eventMessage);
    }
    // Optionally, you can add a toVonage() method for Laravel
9+.
}
```

In the above code, the **via()** method ensures that the notification is sent both as an email and an SMS. The **toMail()** method constructs the email using Laravel's MailMessage, while the **toNexmo()** method builds an SMS using Nexmo's driver.

Configuring Environment Variables for SMS Notifications

To allow Laravel's notification system to send SMS messages, you must configure the SMS driver's credentials. For the built-in Nexmo SMS channel, you need to access and open the **.env** file and add the following lines:

```
# For Nexmo SMS notifications (Laravel 8 or earlier):
NEXMO_KEY=your-nexmo-key
NEXMO_SECRET=your-nexmo-secret
NEXMO_SMS_FROM=your-sender-number
# For Laravel 9+ using Vonage:
VONAGE_KEY=your-vonage-key
VONAGE_SECRET=your-vonage-secret
VONAGE_SMS_FROM=your-sender-number
```

Just insert the actual credentials and then you can observe that these values ensure that when the notification system attempts to send an SMS, it can authenticate with the carrier service.

Sending Test Notification

Now we move on to modifying one of your controller methods, such that it triggers the **ImportantEventNotification** when a critical event occurs. For example, in your **DashboardController**, you can add a method to send the notification:

```
<?php
namespace App\Http\Controllers;
use App\Notifications\ImportantEventNotification;
use Illuminate\Http\Request;
class DashboardController extends Controller
{
    public function alertUser()
    {
        $user = auth()->user();
        // Define the event message and additional details.
        $eventMessage = 'Your account has a critical update.
Please review it immediately.';
        $eventDetails = ['Security Issue', 'Action Required'];
```

```
        // Trigger the notification.
        $user->notify(new
ImportantEventNotification($eventMessage, $eventDetails));
        // Provide feedback to the user or redirect.
        return redirect()->back()->with('status',
'Notification sent successfully!');
    }
}
```

In the above code, when the **alertUser** method is invoked, the currently authenticated user receives an email and an SMS notification. The notification contains a subject, greeting, message details, and a call-to-action in the email, while the SMS carries a concise alert.

While the demonstration above shows a basic implementation, you can customize the notifications further to suit your needs. You might include dynamic data, links for immediate action, or even attach files if required. The flexibility of Laravel's Notification system means that you can evolve these alerts without adding heavy external dependencies—making use of the built-in mail and SMS channels for comprehensive real-time communication.

Additionally, if your user base grows significantly, you may opt to queue these notifications to improve performance. Laravel supports queueing notifications out-of-the-box. To enable this, simply implement the **ShouldQueue** interface in your notification class:

```
use Illuminate\Contracts\Queue\ShouldQueue;
class ImportantEventNotification extends Notification
implements ShouldQueue
{
    // Your notification logic remains the same.
}
```

Be sure to configure your queue driver (such as **database** or **redis**) in your **.env** file to manage the performance impact efficiently. Through this recipe, you have learned how to define, configure, and test a dual-channel notification solution that efficiently alerts users about important events using email and SMS.

Recipe 3: Integrating Real-time Push Notifications

For now, we've got in-app alerts, email, and SMS notifications to keep your users in the loop. But users have said they want to see notifications delivered right away, even when they're not actively refreshing the page. So, to deal with this, you decided to use push notifications with Laravel's broadcasting features, using Laravel Echo along with a service like Pusher. This setup will allow events to be pushed in real time to the client's browser.

Configuring Broadcasting

To begin with this, at first, you need to configure your Laravel application to use Pusher for broadcasting. For this, you need to add the following configuration values, replacing the placeholders with your actual Pusher credentials in your **`.env`** file:

```
BROADCAST_DRIVER=pusher

PUSHER_APP_ID=your-pusher-app-id

PUSHER_APP_KEY=your-pusher-app-key

PUSHER_APP_SECRET=your-pusher-app-secret

PUSHER_APP_CLUSTER=your-pusher-app-cluster
```

These settings tell Laravel to use Pusher as the broadcasting service. Laravel's built-in support for Pusher means that minimal additional setup is required. Next, we then try to verify your broadcasting configuration in **`config/broadcasting.php`** for which we have to ensure that the **`pusher`** connection is properly configured. Typically, it should look like this:

```
'pusher' => [
    'driver' => 'pusher',
    'key' => env('PUSHER_APP_KEY'),
    'secret' => env('PUSHER_APP_SECRET'),
    'app_id' => env('PUSHER_APP_ID'),
    'options' => [
        'cluster' => env('PUSHER_APP_CLUSTER'),
        'useTLS' => true,
    ],
],
```

Laravel will now use these settings to establish a connection with Pusher for broadcasting events.

Creating and Broadcasting Event

To show how real-time push notifications work, we will create a custom event. For example, let's say we want to let users know when a new chat message comes in. Here, we just run the Artisan command:

```
php artisan make:event NewChatMessage
```

This command generates a new event class in the **`app/Events`** directory called **`NewChatMessage.php`**. Now we want to implement this event for which we need to open the generated file **`app/Events/NewChatMessage.php`** and update it to implement the ShouldBroadcast interface. After doing this, it makes the event broadcastable.

Your event class shall be looking like this:

```
<?php
namespace App\Events;
use Illuminate\Broadcasting\Channel;
use Illuminate\Queue\SerializesModels;
use Illuminate\Broadcasting\InteractsWithSockets;
use Illuminate\Contracts\Broadcasting\ShouldBroadcast;
class NewChatMessage implements ShouldBroadcast
{
    use InteractsWithSockets, SerializesModels;
    public $message;
    public $sender;
    /**
     * Create a new event instance.
     *
     * @param string $message
     * @param string $sender
     * @return void
     */
    public function __construct($message, $sender)
    {
        $this->message = $message;
```

```
        $this->sender = $sender;
    }
    /**
     * Get the channels the event should broadcast on.
     *
     * @return Channel|array
     */
    public function broadcastOn()
    {
        return new Channel('chat');
    }
    /**
     * Customize the broadcast event name.
     *
     * @return string
     */
    public function broadcastAs()
    {
        return 'new.chat.message';
    }
}
```

Here, in the above, the event carries a message and sender information. It is broadcast on a public channel named "chat" and is identified by the event name "**new.chat.message**."

Now we try to trigger the event for which, in one of your controller methods (for example, in a ChatController), we try to fire the event when a new chat message is created by changing the controller file as below:

```
<?php
namespace App\Http\Controllers;
use App\Events\NewChatMessage;
use Illuminate\Http\Request;
```

```
class ChatController extends Controller
{
    public function sendMessage(Request $request)
    {
        $message = $request->input('message');
        $sender = auth()->user()->name;
        // Fire the event to broadcast the chat message.
        event(new NewChatMessage($message, $sender));
        // Optionally, return a JSON response.
        return response()->json(['status' => 'Message sent and
broadcasted!']);
    }
}
```

When this method is invoked, the event is fired and broadcast through Pusher, making it available to all clients subscribed to the "chat" channel.

Setting up Laravel Echo

Installing Laravel Echo and Pusher JS

We will need to install both Laravel Echo and the Pusher JavaScript library. In your project's root, run:

```
npm install --save laravel-echo pusher-js
```

After installation, compile your assets using:

```
npm run dev
```

This will update your JavaScript bundle with Laravel Echo and Pusher.

Configuring Laravel Echo

In your JavaScript bootstrap file (typically **resources/js/bootstrap.js**), we try to set up Laravel Echo in which we add the following configuration:

```
import Echo from 'laravel-echo';
```

```
window.Pusher = require('pusher-js');
window.Echo = new Echo({
    broadcaster: 'pusher',
    key: process.env.MIX_PUSHER_APP_KEY, // Ensure that these
environment variables are properly set in your .env and mix
file
    cluster: process.env.MIX_PUSHER_APP_CLUSTER,
    forceTLS: true
});
```

Now here, we must ensure that the corresponding environment variables (**MIX_PUSHER_APP_KEY** and **MIX_PUSHER_APP_CLUSTER**) are defined in your **.env** file and that your **webpack.mix.js** is set to copy these variables into your JavaScript bundle.

Broadcast Event Listening

To do this, make use of Laravel Echo in our javascript file to subscribe to the "chat" channel and listen for the "**new.chat.message**" event:

```
window.Echo.channel('chat')
    .listen('.new.chat.message', (e) => {
        console.log('New chat message received:', e);


        // Optionally, update the UI with the new message.
        let messageElement = document.createElement('div');
        messageElement.innerHTML =
`<strong>${e.sender}:</strong> ${e.message}`;
        document.getElementById('chat-
messages').appendChild(messageElement);
        // For a visual cue, you can trigger a push
notification sound or a UI alert.
        // Example: display a toast notification
        // showToastNotification(`New message from
${e.sender}: ${e.message}`);
    });
```

Now in your Blade view (for example, **resources/views/chat.blade.php**), we need to make saure that we have an element with the ID **chat-messages** where the messages will be appended:

```
<!DOCTYPE html>
<html lang="en">
<head>
    <meta charset="UTF-8">
    <title>Chat Room</title>
    <link rel="stylesheet" href="/css/app.css">
</head>
<body>
    <div id="chat-messages">
        <!-- Existing chat messages will appear here -->
    </div>
    <script src="/js/app.js"></script>
</body>
</html>
```

This above setup means that every time a new chat message is broadcast from your server, the client-side JavaScript listens for the event, logs it to the console, and dynamically updates the chat interface with the new message.

Recipe 4: Monitoring System Performance Metrics

So now from this point, you've got to start keeping a close eye on how your app is performing. This'll help you make sure it can handle more traffic and data processing loads without breaking a sweat. When you did your stress tests recently, you saw that some requests were taking longer than expected and your database queries were using a lot of memory. These performance issues mean you've got to keep a close eye on key metrics like execution times, memory usage, and query loads.

Launching Laravel Telescope

We start with verifiying that you've already published Telescope's assets. If not, then we try the following:

```
php artisan telescope:install
php artisan migrate
```

This creates the necessary tables and config files. After this, we open the browser and navigate to:

```
http://127.0.0.1:8000/telescope
```

This dashboard provides a comprehensive view of HTTP requests, queries, exceptions, and more.

System-Level Metrics

While Telescope and Debugbar focus on application-level performance, you can also check system-level metrics on your Linux server as supplementary confirmation. To do this, first open a separate terminal window and run the following commands:

```
top
```

This shows real-time CPU and memory usage across processes.

```
htop
```

If htop is installed, it provides a more visual representation of resource usage.

```
sudo iotop -o
```

This command monitors disk I/O in real time (if available).

While Telescope and Debugbar capture the application metrics, use **`top`** or **`htop`** in a separate terminal window to see if your CPU load or memory consumption spikes correspond with the slow requests. For real-time comparisons, note down the application metrics from Telescope and match them against your system-level readings.

Conclusion

In this chapter, you put together a full system for alerts, notifications, and performance monitoring in "myapp." You set up in-app alerts using Laravel's Notification system with the database channel, making sure that critical events were instantly visible to users. You set up email and text notifications using Laravel's built-in notification features. You also used Nexmo (or Vonage) credentials to send SMS alerts and customized email content using the MailMessage class. You also integrated push notifications using Laravel Broadcasting with Pusher and Laravel Echo, enabling real-time updates to be sent directly to the client's browser.

Then, you used Laravel Telescope and Laravel Debugbar to keep an eye on system performance metrics like request durations, memory usage, and database query loads. This gave you some great insights into how the application and server were performing. During these steps, you used the tools already installed in your environment, managed via PhpStorm in a Linux setup, to streamline your development process and ensure efficient troubleshooting. This all-in-one approach lets your team keep an eye on how well the app is working, fix problems quickly, and make the user experience better by keeping an eye on performance in a proactive way.

Chapter 7: Job Queues and Background Processes

Overview

In this chapter, you are going to explore the job queues and background processes to enhance the performance and reliability of "myapp." You will begin by learning to configure queue drivers so that heavy tasks—such as sending bulk emails or processing large data sets—are offloaded from the main request cycle. You are going to create custom job classes that encapsulate complex business logic, enabling asynchronous processing and non-blocking execution. Furthermore, you will implement robust retry strategies to manage transient errors and log job failures for easier troubleshooting.

In addition to handling individual jobs, you will explore automating recurring tasks using Laravel Scheduler, ensuring that routine maintenance operations run automatically without manual intervention. Throughout this chapter, you practice live through dispatching, monitoring, and processing background tasks using Linux commands and Laravel's built-in tools along with the essential techniques to maintain a highly responsive application even under heavy load.

Recipe 1: Configuring Queue Drivers

Let us say that we observed some heavy tasks—such as sending large batches of emails, processing image uploads, or generating extensive reports—were directly executed within HTTP requests. This slowed down the user experience but and also impacted overall application responsiveness. Now, to overcome these challenges, we can try to offload such tasks to background processes using Laravel's job queues. Queue drivers allow you to dispatch tasks asynchronously, so they're executed separately from the main request-response cycle. This decoupling of tasks results in a faster, more responsive application and a smoother user experience. So now, you will learn what queue drivers are and how to set them up using Laravel's built-in functionality along with Linux commands, ensuring that heavy tasks are efficiently managed in the background.

Configuring Queue Driver

Queue drivers in Laravel enable you to offload and process time-consuming tasks asynchronously. Instead of executing these tasks during a user request—leading to slow responses—tasks are pushed onto a queue and processed later by a dedicated worker. This is extremely useful for tasks like sending emails, processing videos, or interfacing with third-party APIs. Laravel supports multiple queue drivers like database, Redis, Beanstalkd, and Amazon SQS. For simplicity and leveraging existing infrastructure, we will use the database queue driver in this demonstration. The database driver uses a table in your existing database to store queued jobs, making it an excellent choice for development and small-scale production environments.

Set Queue Connection

You can set the queue connection to database by adding or editing the following line:

```
QUEUE_CONNECTION=database
```

This instructs Laravel to use the database queue driver, which stores job entries in a dedicated table.

Create Jobs Table

The Laravel requires a table to store the queued jobs when using the database driver. For this, you can generate the migration file for the jobs table by running:

```
php artisan queue:table
```

This command creates a migration file in **database/migrations** for the jobs table.

Run Migration

Then apply the migration to update your database with the required table:

```
php artisan migrate
```

This command will create the **jobs** table in your database where Laravel will record each queued job.

Dispatching Job to Queue

Create Sample Job

We need a sample job to simulate a heavy task that you want to process in the background. And for this, you need to generate a new job class called **ProcessHeavyTask**:

```
php artisan make:job ProcessHeavyTask
```

This creates a new file in **app/Jobs/ProcessHeavyTask.php**.

Implement Job Logic

Now, open **ProcessHeavyTask.php** and update it to include logic that simulates heavy processing. Here, you can use a sleep command to mimic a long-running task:

```
<?php
namespace App\Jobs;
use Illuminate\Bus\Queueable;
use Illuminate\Contracts\Queue\ShouldQueue;
```

```
use Illuminate\Foundation\Bus\Dispatchable;
use Illuminate\Queue\InteractsWithQueue;
use Illuminate\Queue\SerializesModels;
class ProcessHeavyTask implements ShouldQueue
{
    use Dispatchable, InteractsWithQueue, Queueable,
SerializesModels;
    /**
     * Execute the job.
     *
     * @return void
     */
    public function handle()
    {
        // Simulate a heavy processing task
        sleep(10); // Simulates a delay of 10 seconds
        \Log::info('ProcessHeavyTask executed successfully.');
    }
}
```

Dispatch Job

In one of your controller methods (for instance, in **DashboardController**), dispatch this job to the queue:

```
<?php
namespace App\Http\Controllers;
use App\Jobs\ProcessHeavyTask;
use Illuminate\Http\Request;
class DashboardController extends Controller
{
    public function triggerHeavyTask()
```

```
    {
        // Dispatch the heavy task to the queue
        ProcessHeavyTask::dispatch();
        return response()->json(['message' => 'Heavy task
dispatched successfully.']);
    }
}
```

This code offloads the heavy task, ensuring the user's request is processed quickly while the task runs in the background.

Processing Queue with Linux Commands

Starting Queue Worker

To process queued jobs, you must run the queue worker. In your Linux terminal within the "myapp" directory, you then execute:

```
php artisan queue:work
```

This command starts processing jobs from the **`jobs`** table. As jobs are dispatched, the worker picks them up and executes the **`handle()`** method.

Monitoring Worker

Keep the terminal session running to monitor the worker's output. You should see log messages confirming that your heavy task was processed. If you wish to stop the worker, simply press **`Ctrl + C`**.

For production environments, try using a process manager like Supervisor to manage your queue workers automatically. However, for this demonstration, running the command manually is sufficient.

You can follow the below Supervisor configuration snippet:

```
[program:laravel_queue_worker]
process_name=%(program_name)s_%(process_num)02d
command=php /path/to/myapp/artisan queue:work --sleep=3 --
tries=3
autostart=true
```

```
autorestart=true
user=your_linux_user
numprocs=1
redirect_stderr=true
stdout_logfile=/path/to/myapp/storage/logs/queue.log
```

With this, you learned what queue drivers are and how they help offload heavy tasks, thereby improving your application's responsiveness. You set the queue connection to 'database,' created the required migration, and dispatched a sample job that simulates a heavy task. And then, you processed the queued job using Linux commands, confirming the successful offloading and execution of tasks in the background.

Recipe 2: Creating Custom Job Classes

Now, let's say you're dealing with a situation where certain business processes—like generating comprehensive reports or processing large datasets—need to run asynchronously to avoid messing with the user experience. Your team decided that moving these tasks to the background would make operations more efficient and improve responsiveness. To do this, you decided to put different business logic into custom job classes that would run asynchronously. This approach makes sure that your main application stays responsive while heavy or time-consuming tasks run in the background. Now, we will learn how to create and configure custom job classes for asynchronous processing using Laravel's job system, optimize task automation, and maintain efficiency.

Creating Custom Job Class

Generating Job Class

First, we need to start by generating a custom job class with an Artisan command. And for this, simply run the following:

```
php artisan make:job GenerateReportJob
```

This creates a new job class file at **app/Jobs/GenerateReportJob.php** that you will use to encapsulate the report generation logic.

Implementing Job Logic

Next, open the **GenerateReportJob.php** and update the class to include the necessary logic to process the report asynchronously. Try to understand from the following sample program:

```php
<?php
namespace App\Jobs;
use Illuminate\Bus\Queueable;
use Illuminate\Contracts\Queue\ShouldQueue;
use Illuminate\Foundation\Bus\Dispatchable;
use Illuminate\Queue\InteractsWithQueue;
use Illuminate\Queue\SerializesModels;
class GenerateReportJob implements ShouldQueue
{
    use Dispatchable, InteractsWithQueue, Queueable,
SerializesModels;
    protected $reportId;
    /**
     * Create a new job instance.
     *
     * @param int $reportId
     * @return void
     */
    public function __construct($reportId)
    {
        $this->reportId = $reportId;
    }
    /**
     * Execute the job.
     *
     * @return void
     */
    public function handle()
    {
```

```
        // Simulate heavy report generation logic
        \Log::info("Starting report generation for report ID: {$this->reportId}");

        // Simulated delay to represent processing time
        sleep(10);

        // Here you would include the actual report generation code,
        // like querying the database, performing calculations, and saving the report.
        \Log::info("Completed report generation for report ID: {$this->reportId}");
    }
}
```

Here, the job accepts a report identifier and simulates a time-consuming task using **`sleep(10)`**.

Dispatching Custom Job

In a controller method say, within **`ReportController`**—you can dispatch this job to the queue. To do this, you need to add a method to trigger the report generation in your controller file as shown below:

```
<?php
namespace App\Http\Controllers;
use App\Jobs\GenerateReportJob;
use Illuminate\Http\Request;
class ReportController extends Controller
{
    public function generateReport(Request $request)
    {
        // Assume a report identifier is passed as input
        $reportId = $request->input('report_id', 1);
```

```
        // Dispatch the report generation job to the queue
        GenerateReportJob::dispatch($reportId);
        // Respond quickly to the user indicating the process
has started
        return response()->json(['message' => 'Report
generation initiated. It will be available shortly.']);
    }
}
```

This above dispatches **GenerateReportJob** with the given report ID, and the job is placed on the queue and processed asynchronously, keeping the HTTP request-response cycle fast.

Processing Custom Job

Now here, to process the queued job, you need to run the queue worker by executing:

```
php artisan queue:work
```

This starts the worker, which listens for and processes jobs from the **jobs** table.

After dispatching the job through your controller, monitor the terminal output running the queue worker. You should see log messages indicating that the report generation process has started and completed. Additionally, check your **storage/logs/laravel.log** file to confirm that the logs generated within your job are recorded.

This whole approach offloads heavy tasks to background processes, ensuring non-blocking execution, and maintaining a responsive application.

Recipe 3: Managing Job Failures

Now, let's say you run into some annoying issues where jobs sent for background processing sometimes fail without any obvious fix. For example, during an update to generate reports asynchronously, some jobs never finished because of temporary network errors or short-lived database connectivity issues. It's possible that the reason for the issue is that there's no retry strategy in place, which has led to some operations being incomplete. There's also been a lack of proper error logging, which has made it hard to understand what the problems are. We could try to solve this by using Laravel's built-in retry strategies and failure logging to manage job failures. Today, we will learn how to capture failed jobs, set retry limits for transient errors, and make sure that job failures are properly logged and managed so that your background tasks run reliably.

Configuring Retry Strategy in Job Class

The Laravel allows you to define how many times a job should be attempted before being marked as failed. So, we simply access the custom job class (**GenerateReportJob** created earlier) and set properties to define retry behavior. In the job class, we add properties for retry attempts and timeout as shown below:

```
<?php
namespace App\Jobs;
use Exception;
use Illuminate\Bus\Queueable;
use Illuminate\Contracts\Queue\ShouldQueue;
use Illuminate\Foundation\Bus\Dispatchable;
use Illuminate\Queue\InteractsWithQueue;
use Illuminate\Queue\SerializesModels;
class GenerateReportJob implements ShouldQueue
{
    use Dispatchable, InteractsWithQueue, Queueable,
SerializesModels;
    protected $reportId;
    public $tries = 5; // Attempt the job up to 5 times before
failing.
    public $timeout = 120; // Job should timeout after 120
seconds.
    /**
     * Create a new job instance.
     *
     * @param int $reportId
     * @return void
     */
    public function __construct($reportId)
    {
        $this->reportId = $reportId;
    }
```

```
    /**
     * Execute the job.
     *
     * @return void
     */
    public function handle()
    {
        try {
            \Log::info("Starting report generation for report
ID: {$this->reportId}");
            // Simulated heavy task using sleep
            sleep(10);
            // Simulate potential transient error: (For
example, randomly fail)
            if (rand(1, 3) === 1) {
                throw new Exception("Simulated transient error
during report generation.");
            }
            \Log::info("Completed report generation for report
ID: {$this->reportId}");
        } catch (Exception $e) {
            \Log::error("Error in GenerateReportJob for report
ID: {$this->reportId}: " . $e->getMessage());
            // Re-throw exception so that Laravel handles the
retry
            throw $e;
        }
    }
}
```

In the above script,

- The **$tries** property ensures that the job is retried up to five times before it is marked as failed.

- The **$timeout** property sets the maximum time allowed for the job to run.
- Within the **handle()** method, transient errors are simulated and captured. So, if an exception occurs, the job logs the error and re-throws it so that Laravel's queue system can attempt a retry.

Monitoring and Logging Failed Jobs

The Laravel automatically logs failed jobs in the **failed_jobs** table. We can create such table by running:

```
php artisan queue:failed-table
php artisan migrate
```

After this, any job that exhausts its retry attempts gets recorded in the **failed_jobs** table. You can view failed jobs by running:

```
php artisan queue:failed
```

This command lists jobs that have failed along with the error messages that caused the failure and the detailed logs can be found in **storage/logs/laravel.log**.

Customizing Failure Handling

The Laravel allows you to define a **failed()** method on your job class. This method is executed when the job has failed permanently after all retry attempts are exhausted. In your **GenerateReportJob** class, we can add a **failed()** method to handle such cases:

```
public function failed(Exception $exception)
{
    // Here you can send notifications, log extra details, or perform other cleanup actions
    \Log::critical("Job permanently failed for report ID: {$this->reportId}. Exception: " . $exception->getMessage());
    // Optionally, send an alert to the admin team using the Notification system
    // $admin = User::where('role', 'admin')->first();
    // $admin->notify(new JobFailureNotification($this->reportId, $exception->getMessage()));
```

```
}
```

This method helps you execute specific tasks when a job fails permanently. For example, you might notify administrators or trigger a specific workflow for further investigation.

Handling Transient Errors Effectively

The retry mechanism in Laravel's job system is particularly useful for handling transient errors, such as intermittent database connectivity issues or temporary API downtime. In the **handle()** method, by re-throwing exceptions, you let the framework automatically retry the job. You can also implement conditional logic to decide not to retry for fatal errors by adding custom conditions within your **failed()** method or even within the **handle()** method before deciding to rethrow an exception.

For example, you might add additional logging or a custom delay before retries for certain errors. Laravel allows you to customize retry delays by overriding the **retryUntil()** method if necessary:

```
public function retryUntil()
{
    // Retry until 1 hour from now
    return now()->addHour();
}
```

This function defines how long the job should keep retrying before it is considered as permanently failed.

Testing Retry Mechanism

So here, we first try to trigger the job. To do this, in your **ReportController**, we dispatch the **GenerateReportJob**:

```
public function generateReport(Request $request)
{
    $reportId = $request->input('report_id', 1);
    GenerateReportJob::dispatch($reportId);
    return response()->json(['message' => 'Report generation
initiated.']);
}
```

Since our sample job includes a random error throw, we need to repeatedly trigger the job until you see it retried. And while you do, you keep monitoring the terminal where you run the queue worker:

```
php artisan queue:work
```

You should see log messages from the worker indicating retries. After exhausting retries, the job will be recorded in the **failed_jobs** table.

After this, check the log file to confirm that errors were logged appropriately and then run:

```
php artisan queue:failed
```

This should list the job along with the error message after it has permanently failed. This whole setup ensured that heavy background tasks would not block the application indefinitely and provided your development team with detailed logs for troubleshooting persistent issues.

Recipe 4: Automating Recurring Tasks

Whether it is cleaning up logs, sending out weekly summaries, or refreshing cache data, all such recurring tasks need to be executed reliably without manual intervention. And we want to automate these tasks to improve efficiency and also to reduce human error. To achieve this, you decided to implement Laravel's built-in Scheduler, which can schedule and run recurring tasks automatically. So here, we will try to leverage Laravel Scheduler to define and execute recurring tasks seamlessly. This integration will enable to automate routine operations such as database maintenance, cleanup procedures, and regular report generation, all without the need to run repetitive manual commands.

Configuring Scheduler

The Laravel Scheduler allows you to fluently and expressively schedule command execution within your Laravel application. It provides a single, convenient API for defining scheduled tasks inside the **App\Console\Kernel.php** file. The scheduler is designed to work hand in hand with Linux's cron system; you only need to set up one cron entry that runs every minute to allow Laravel's scheduler to handle the rest.

Now to begin, first open the **Kernel.php** file wherein you will see a **schedule()** method, which is where all scheduled tasks are defined. Here, you can schedule commands, closures, and even callable functions.

So now, we define a recurring task that clears old logs daily. For this, we add the following code to the **schedule()** method inside the **Kernel** class:

```
protected function schedule(Schedule $schedule)
```

```
{
    // Clear application logs daily at midnight.
    $schedule->command('logs:clear')->daily();
    // Optionally, you can schedule other tasks, for example:
    // $schedule->command('backup:run')->weekly();
    // $schedule->call(function () {
    //     // Some custom task logic
    // })->everyThirtyMinutes();
}
```

In the above, the **logs:clear** command is scheduled to run daily at midnight. You can define your own commands or closures as needed. The Scheduler provides many fluent methods like **daily()**, **weekly()**, **hourly()**, and custom CRON expressions using **cron('expression')** to allow complete flexibility.

Creating Custom Artisan Command

Generating Command

The Laravel Scheduler can run any Artisan command and so we start to create a custom Artisan command that clears old logs as below:

```
php artisan make:command ClearLogs
```

This creates a new command file in **app/Console/Commands/ClearLogs.php**.

Implementing Command Logic

Now, lets access to the **ClearLogs.php** and update the class to implement the logic for clearing logs with below:

```
<?php
namespace App\Console\Commands;
use Illuminate\Console\Command;
use Illuminate\Support\Facades\File;
class ClearLogs extends Command
{
```

```
    /**
     * The name and signature of the console command.
     *
     * @var string
     */
    protected $signature = 'logs:clear';
    /**
     * The console command description.
     *
     * @var string
     */
    protected $description = 'Clear the log files in the
storage/logs directory';
    /**
     * Execute the console command.
     *
     * @return int
     */
    public function handle()
    {
        $logPath = storage_path('logs');

        // Delete all log files except for .gitignore
        $files = File::files($logPath);
        foreach ($files as $file) {
            if ($file->getFilename() !== '.gitignore') {
                File::delete($file->getRealPath());
            }
        }
        $this->info('Logs have been cleared successfully!');
```

```
        return 0;
    }
}
```

Here in the above snippet, the job is to iterate through the **storage/logs** directory and delete all log files except the **.gitignore** file. When executed, it prints a confirmation message to the console. This is a straightforward example of how you can define custom job logic to perform routine maintenance.

Testing Custom Command Manually

Before integrating the command with the Scheduler, test it manually by running:

```
php artisan logs:clear
```

The output should indicate that the logs have been cleared successfully. Check your **storage/logs** directory afterward to verify that the log files were deleted.

Scheduling Custom Command

The Laravel Scheduler requires a single cron entry to execute the **schedule:run** command every minute. This entry triggers the Scheduler, which in turn executes all tasks that are due. Now to do this, you edit your crontab with following change to the crontab file:

```
crontab -e
* * * * * cd /path/to/myapp && php artisan schedule:run >>
/dev/null 2>&1
```

This line ensures that every minute, Laravel checks for due tasks as defined in **Kernel.php** and executes them accordingly.

Now, to verify that your scheduled tasks are running, you can monitor the Laravel log file. Another approach is to modify the **ClearLogs** command temporarily to log a message each time it runs, then wait for the next scheduled minute and check if the message appears.

Advanced Scheduler Features

The Laravel Scheduler supports custom CRON expressions, giving you complete control over the frequency of task execution. For example, if you need a task to run every five minutes, you can define:

```
$schedule->command('reports:generate')->cron('*/5 * * * *');
```

This flexibility let you to fine-tune how often tasks run based on your application's requirements and server capacity. As your application grows, you can add multiple commands and even closure-based tasks to the Scheduler in **Kernel.php** as below:

```
protected function schedule(Schedule $schedule)
{
    // Clear logs every day at midnight
    $schedule->command('logs:clear')->daily();

    // Generate a summary report every Monday at 8 AM
    $schedule->command('reports:generate')->weeklyOn(1,
'8:00');

    // Execute a custom closure every thirty minutes
    $schedule->call(function () {
        // Custom task logic here
    })->everyThirtyMinutes();
}
```

With such centralization of these tasks, you can easily reduce manual maintenance of your application.

So, with this, you learned to define scheduled tasks in the **Kernel.php** file, create a custom Artisan command for clearing logs, and configure a Linux cron job to trigger the Scheduler every minute. This setup ensures that routine maintenance operations, such as clearing logs or generating reports, run automatically without manual intervention.

Summary

In this chapter, you configured Laravel's job queue system to offload heavy tasks from the main application flow and improve responsiveness in "myapp." You started by setting up the queue driver using the database connection in your .env file and creating the necessary migration for the jobs table. Then, you built a custom job class—GenerateReportJob—to encapsulate business logic for asynchronous processing. This made sure that tasks like report generation didn't block user requests. You put in place retry strategies and managed job failures by defining properties like $tries and $timeout, and by using the failed() method to log errors and handle transient issues. You can finally automate those pesky recurring tasks by taking advantage of Laravel Scheduler.

Just integrate it with Linux cron, and it'll take care of the maintenance commands for you, like clearing logs or generating those periodic reports. You can combine these techniques with some practical testing using Linux commands and tools like PhpStorm and Laravel Debugbar. This'll streamline background processing, enhance reliability, and optimize resource usage without affecting the application's performance. This all-inclusive approach made sure that the heavy lifting was done efficiently in the background, and detailed logs and monitoring gave us a heads-up on any issues that popped up.

Chapter 8: File Storage, Media Management, and Processing

Overview

In this chapter, we will learn how to manage file storage and media processing in the application effectively. We will learn how to keep your media files safe and sound on your Linux server by setting up some dedicated storage disks in Laravel's filesystem. You're going to learn how to set up secure file upload mechanisms that include strong validation procedures to make sure that only files that meet the requirements are accepted.

In addition, we will integrate the Intervention Image library to automate image processing tasks like resizing, cropping, and optimizing images. This ensures that media files are both performance-friendly and securely stored. We will also learn how to use Laravel's built-in response methods to stream and download files efficiently. It helps with the high-traffic scenarios and reduce server load. This chapter is meant to give you the know-how to keep your media assets safe and optimize them to get the best performance. It'll also show you how to integrate media management into your application's workflow, making sure your security is solid and the user experience is top-notch.

Recipe 1: Configuring Local Media Storage

In your app you reached a point where handling media files securely on your Linux server became critical for both security and efficiency. Your application deals with sensitive user-uploaded images and documents, which require a protected file storage solution that isolates media files from the public directory and restricts unauthorized access. Now that you recognized the need for a robust system to configure storage paths, control file access permissions, and ensure that your media handling routines operate within a secure environment. So here, you will work towards to configure local storage for media files exclusively on your Linux server, detail the necessary configuration steps in Laravel's settings, and apply Linux commands to secure the storage directories. This teaches you to set up designated storage paths, have the correct folder permissions, and ultimately provide secure access to media assets within our "myapp."

Configuring Storage Paths

The Laravel uses a unified API for file storage that supports local disks, cloud-based disks, and more through the Filesystem abstraction. In our case, we will focus on local storage. The default disk configuration is defined in the **config/filesystems.php** file, where Laravel defines the default disk as "local" and provides settings for the "public" disk. By default, files are stored in the **storage/app** directory with public files typically served via symbolic links in **public/storage**. However, you can configure alternative storage paths and customize the disk configuration to meet your application's security needs.

So to begin with, first open the file **config/filesystems.php** in PhpStorm. Here, we will see a configuration array for disks. The default "local" disk is typically defined as:

```
'local' => [
    'driver' => 'local',
    'root' => storage_path('app'),
],
```

Now to manage media files securely, you might create a new disk specifically for media assets. So just add a new disk configuration in the **disks** array:

```
'media' => [
    'driver' => 'local',
    'root' => storage_path('app/media'),
    'visibility' => 'private',
],
```

In the above config, you define a dedicated disk named **media** that stores files in the **storage/app/media** directory. The **visibility** parameter is set to **private**, ensuring that files on this disk are not publicly accessible by default.

Now, we have to create a media directory as below:

```
mkdir -p storage/app/media
```

Securing File Access

Setting Linux File Permissions

For secure file storage, you want to ensure that the media directory is only accessible to the web server user (typically **www-data** on Linux) and the application itself. This prevents unauthorized access from other users on the system.

Now here, you can change the ownership of the media directory to the web server user by doing the following:

```
sudo chown -R www-data:www-data storage/app/media
```

This assigns the web server user and group (**www-data**) as the owner of the media directory and all its contents. We can then set the appropriate permissions to ensure the directory is readable and writable by the owner, and not accessible by others:

```
sudo chmod -R 700 storage/app/media
```

The **700** permission grants full access to the owner while denying access to group and others. If your application architecture requires group sharing, you might adjust this to **750** (owner full access, group read/execute, others no access).

Configuring Public Access

Now here, if you require controlled public access (for example, for user avatars), you might use Laravel's **storage:link** command with additional security measures siuch as, if you decide to serve some media files publicly, run:

```
php artisan storage:link
```

This command creates a symbolic link from **public/storage** to **storage/app/public**. However, in our case, we are using the **media** disk configured as private. If you need to serve a subset of files from media with controlled access, consider creating a dedicated controller to stream files after checking user permissions instead of a direct symbolic link.

For files intended to be served to end users, create a controller method that retrieves the file from the private media disk and returns it via a response.

```
use Illuminate\Support\Facades\Storage;
public function getMediaFile($filename)
{
    // Ensure that the user is authenticated and authorized to
access the file
    if (!auth()->check()) {
        abort(403);
    }
    $path = 'media/' . $filename;
    if (!Storage::disk('media')->exists($filename)) {
        abort(404);
    }
    return response()->file(Storage::disk('media')-
>path($filename));
}
```

This checks if a media file exists in the private disk and then securely streams it to the user.

Practical Upload and Retrieval Operations

Uploading Media Files to Private Disk

To implement the file upload, we first open the media controller and write an upload method to handle file uploads securely as below:

```
<?php
namespace App\Http\Controllers;
use Illuminate\Http\Request;
use Illuminate\Support\Facades\Storage;
class MediaController extends Controller
{
    public function upload(Request $request)
    {
        // Validate the file upload
        $validatedData = $request->validate([
            'file' => 'required|file|max:10240', // Limit the
file size to 10MB
        ]);
        // Store the file in the 'media' disk
        $file = $request->file('file');
        $filename = time() . '_' . $file-
>getClientOriginalName();
        $filePath = $file->storeAs('', $filename, 'media');
        // Optionally, store the file path in the database
associated with the user or a record
        return response()->json(['message' => 'File uploaded
successfully!', 'path' => $filePath]);
    }
}
```

1. This controller method validates the uploaded file, stores it in the configured **`media`** disk, and returns a response with the file path.

Next, we add a route for the file upload endpoint in **routes/web.php**:

```
Route::post('/media/upload',
[App\Http\Controllers\MediaController::class, 'upload'])-
>name('media.upload');
```

This route will be used to trigger the file upload operation.

Retrieving Media Files Securely

As noted earlier, we need to create a method in your **MediaController** to securely retrieve a file as shown below:

```
public function download($filename)
{
    // Validate user authentication or other access rights
here
    if (!auth()->check()) {
        abort(403);
    }
    // Check if the file exists and then stream the file back
    if (!Storage::disk('media')->exists($filename)) {
        abort(404);
    }

    $path = Storage::disk('media')->path($filename);
    return response()->download($path, $filename, [],
'inline');
}
```

Next, we create a route for file retrieval:

```
Route::get('/media/download/{filename}',
[App\Http\Controllers\MediaController::class, 'download'])-
>name('media.download');
```

Now to do the testing, we upload a file via an API client like Postman or a simple HTML form.

We then verify that the file is stored in **storage/app/media** and that appropriate file permissions are set by checking with Linux commands:

```
ls -l storage/app/media
```

Verifying System Security

Now here, after configuring storage and file upload functionalities, we can easily use the Linux commands to verify permissions and security. For example:

```
ls -l storage/app/media
```

Optionally, you can create bash scripts to monitor and log any changes in the media storage directory. This can be scheduled using Linux cron jobs to run periodic security audits.

All these detailed steps get us the secured local storage for media files in our "myapp." Furthermore, you implemented practical file upload and retrieval operations with the help of Laravel controllers and routes, ensuring that media files are uploaded securely and streamed to authenticated users.

Recipe 2: Automating Image Processing and Optimization

As your app got bigger, you realized that processing images was becoming super important. It was essential to manage image files effectively, whether for user-uploaded photos, product images, or profile pictures. Your team talked about how automating tasks like resizing, cropping, and improving image quality could boost performance and give users a more consistent experience. You decided to use the Intervention Image library to deal with this issue. It's a solid solution for handling images in PHP. This'll let your app adjust images based on predefined dimensions and quality parameters, making sure all images are stored and displayed properly.

Installing Intervention Image Library

We can easily install the Intervention Image package using composer as below:

```
composer require intervention/image
```

However, if you are on an earlier version or need manual registration, add the following lines to your **config/app.php**:

In the **providers** array:

```
Intervention\Image\ImageServiceProvider::class,
```

In the **aliases** array:

```
'Image' => Intervention\Image\Facades\Image::class,
```

This sets up the library for use throughout your Laravel application.

Now, this Intervention Image is extremely flexible. You can use it to perform a variety of tasks such as resizing, cropping, and adjusting image quality. For this demonstration, we will focus on resizing and optimizing images. You can define a configuration file if needed, but for most cases the default settings will suffice. The integration allows you to chain image manipulation methods fluently.

Implementing Automated Image Processing

Now here, to demonstrate image processing, we will open our existing controller and add a method that handles an image upload, processes it, and stores the optimized version.

```
<?php
namespace App\Http\Controllers;
use Illuminate\Http\Request;
use Illuminate\Support\Facades\Storage;
use Intervention\Image\Facades\Image;
class MediaController extends Controller
{
    public function uploadAndProcess(Request $request)
    {
        // Validate the file upload, ensuring an image is
provided.
        $request->validate([
            'image' => 'required|image|max:5120', // max size
5MB
        ]);
        // Retrieve the uploaded file
        $file = $request->file('image');
```

```
        // Generate a unique file name with extension
        $filename = time() . '_' . $file-
>getClientOriginalName();
        // Create an image instance from the file using
Intervention Image
        $image = Image::make($file);
        // Resize the image to a maximum width of 800px while
maintaining aspect ratio,
        // you can add constraints to avoid upsizing smaller
images.
        $image->resize(800, null, function ($constraint) {
            $constraint->aspectRatio();
            $constraint->upsize();
        });
        // Optionally, adjust the image quality (e.g., 75%
quality for optimization)
        $quality = 75;
        // Save the processed image to the local media disk we
configured earlier
        // The disk 'media' is assumed to be configured to
store files in storage/app/media
        Storage::disk('media')->put($filename, (string)
$image->encode('jpg', $quality));
        // Optionally, store file path and metadata in the
database if needed
        return response()->json([
            'message' => 'Image processed and uploaded
successfully!',
            'filename' => $filename,
            'path' => Storage::disk('media')->url($filename)
        ]);
    }
```

```
}
```

Here, the method validates that an image file is provided and ensures the file does not exceed 5MB. The uploaded image is captured from the request and a unique filename is generated using the current timestamp. This helps prevent file collisions.

The Intervention Image facade creates an image instance from the uploaded file. The image is then resized to a maximum width of 800 pixels while maintaining the aspect ratio. The upsize constraint prevents small images from being stretched unnecessarily. The image is encoded into JPEG format with reduced quality (75%) to optimize file size while preserving visual quality. Adjust the quality parameter as needed based on your requirements.

Finally, the processed image is stored in the secure local storage disk ("media") defined in your Laravel configuration. This keeps your images isolated from the public directory unless explicitly served via a secure controller.

Setting up Route

To do this, we define a route to handle the image upload and processing. For this, we open the **`routes/web.php`** file and add the following:

```
Route::post('/media/upload-process',
[App\Http\Controllers\MediaController::class,
'uploadAndProcess'])->name('media.upload.process');
```

This route directs POST requests to the **`uploadAndProcess`** method in your **`MediaController`**.

Testing Implementation

Now to test the implementation, we create a simple HTML form to test the image uploads. For example, we create a Blade view (**`resources/views/media/upload.blade.php`**):

```
<!DOCTYPE html>
<html lang="en">
<head>
    <meta charset="UTF-8">
    <title>Upload and Process Image</title>
</head>
<body>
    <h1>Upload an Image</h1>
```

```
    <form action="{{ route('media.upload.process') }}"
method="POST" enctype="multipart/form-data">
        @csrf
        <input type="file" name="image" required>
        <button type="submit">Upload and Process</button>
    </form>
</body>
</html>
```

After this, we open the form in your browser, select an image, and submit the form. After testing, we then navigate to the **storage/app/media** directory and run the following:

```
ls -l storage/app/media
```

While doing this, we need to ensure that the processed image file exists, and verify that the file permissions are set securely as per your previous configuration.

Recipe 3: Enabling File Streaming and Downloads

With time passing by, we may come across situations wherein users frequently requested to stream and download large media files, such as high-resolution images or documents. With increasing traffic, the need to efficiently deliver these files without hampering server performance became critical. Here, we need to implement an optimized file streaming and download mechanism using Laravel's built-in functionalities. So, you will learn how to implement these functionalities such that our application supports file streaming and downloads for end users.

Laravel's File Streaming and Download Capabilities

The Laravel provides built-in response methods—**response()->file()** and **response()->download()**. Both of these allow you to serve files directly from the storage with minimal overhead. The **response()->file()** method displays a file inline in the browser. This method reads the file from disk and sends appropriate headers for inline display, ideal for images, PDFs, or media that users view directly in the browser. And, the **response()->download()** method forces the browser to download the file. It sets the **Content-Disposition** header to **attachment**, optionally allowing you to specify a file name and custom headers.

Both these methods are optimized to handle large files by streaming the file in chunks rather than loading it all into memory at once. And this is of much importance for high-traffic scenarios, as it minimizes server memory usage and improves response times.

Implementing Efficient File Streaming

Creating Controller Method for File Streaming

In your **MediaController**, add a method dedicated to streaming files. This method will retrieve the file from your secure **media** disk and stream it to the client.

```
<?php
namespace App\Http\Controllers;
use Illuminate\Support\Facades\Storage;
use Illuminate\Http\Request;
class MediaController extends Controller
{
    public function streamFile($filename)
    {
        // Check if the requested file exists on the 'media'
disk
        if (!Storage::disk('media')->exists($filename)) {
            abort(404, 'File not found.');
        }
        // Retrieve the full path to the file on disk
        $path = Storage::disk('media')->path($filename);
        // Set headers for caching and content type based on
file extension
        $headers = [
            'Content-Type' => Storage::disk('media')-
>mimeType($filename),
            'Cache-Control' => 'max-age=86400, public', //
Cache file for 1 day
        ];
```

```
        // Stream the file using Laravel's response()->file()
method
        return response()->file($path, $headers);
    }
}
```

Defining Streaming Route

In your **routes/web.php** file, add a route for file streaming:

```
Route::get('/media/stream/{filename}',
[App\Http\Controllers\MediaController::class, 'streamFile'])-
>name('media.stream');
```

Testing File Streaming

Run the Laravel server using:

```
php artisan serve
```

Then, open the web browser and navigate to:

```
http://127.0.0.1:8000/media/stream/yourfilename.jpg
```

The file should be streamed directly in the browser, and caching headers should be set to optimize subsequent requests.

Implementing File Downloads

Creating Controller Method for File Downloads

Next, add another method in your **MediaController** for enabling file downloads. This method forces the file to be downloaded rather than displayed inline.

```
public function downloadFile($filename)
{
    // Verify the file exists on the 'media' disk
    if (!Storage::disk('media')->exists($filename)) {
        abort(404, 'File not found.');
    }
```

```
    // Retrieve the absolute file path
    $path = Storage::disk('media')->path($filename);
    // Optionally, customize headers for downloads
    $headers = [
        'Content-Type' => Storage::disk('media')-
>mimeType($filename),
        'Cache-Control' => 'max-age=86400, public', // Cache
for efficient repeat downloads
    ];
    // Use response()->download() to force the download.
    return response()->download($path, $filename, $headers);
}
```

Defining Download Route

For this, create the route for file downloads in **routes/web.php**:

```
Route::get('/media/download/{filename}',
[App\Http\Controllers\MediaController::class,
'downloadFile'])->name('media.download');
```

Testing Download Functionality

While your Laravel server is running, visit:

```
http://127.0.0.1:8000/media/download/yourfilename.jpg
```

This should initiate a file download in your browser. And keep verifying the correct headers are sent and that the file is downloaded efficiently even under high traffic conditions.

Advanced Techniques for High Traffic Environments

Utilizing Chunked Downloads

For very large files, we can use chunked downloads to further optimize memory usage. Although Laravel's native methods handle chunking well, you may implement further logic if needed. Following is an example using a streamed response:

```
public function downloadFileChunked($filename)
```

```
{
    if (!Storage::disk('media')->exists($filename)) {
        abort(404, 'File not found.');
    }
    $path = Storage::disk('media')->path($filename);
    $mime = Storage::disk('media')->mimeType($filename);
    return response()->streamDownload(function () use ($path)
{
        $stream = fopen($path, 'rb');
        while (!feof($stream)) {
            echo fread($stream, 8192); // Read in 8KB chunks
            flush();
        }
        fclose($stream);
    }, $filename, [
        'Content-Type' => $mime,
        'Cache-Control' => 'max-age=86400, public',
    ]);
}
```

Here, we then define a corresponding route if you wish to test chunked downloads:

```
Route::get('/media/download-chunked/{filename}',
[App\Http\Controllers\MediaController::class,
'downloadFileChunked'])->name('media.download.chunked');
```

This method is useful for serving files that are particularly large, ensuring that the PHP process does not overload its memory limit by processing the file in manageable chunks.

Caching Headers and Content Delivery

To support high traffic, we have to be cautious about caching headers being correctly configured. The above examples include **`Cache-Control`** headers to allow client and intermediary caches (such as CDNs, if introduced) to store files temporarily, reducing load on the server.

With all these detailed steps, you successfully enabled efficient file streaming and downloads in "myapp" by utilizing Laravel's built-in response methods and secure file storage configurations.

Summary

By now, you've got a secure and efficient system for handling media files in your app on your Linux server. You started by setting up local file storage by tweaking Laravel's filesystem configuration to create a special "media" disk with a secure storage path. You used Linux commands to set the right ownership and permissions, making sure that only the web server could access these files. You also put in place solid file upload and retrieval procedures, checking file types and sizes to stop malicious uploads and prevent people from misusing resources. You also integrated the Intervention Image library to automate image processing tasks like resizing and optimizing images for performance, and you demonstrated secure file streaming and download functionalities by leveraging Laravel's response methods.

CHAPTER 9: SCHEDULING, AUTOMATION, AND BACKUP TASKS

Overview

In this chapter, we will discover how to tap into the potential of scheduling, automation, and backup tasks to keep "myapp" running smoothly and efficiently. You're going to learn how to centrally manage recurring tasks by configuring Laravel's Scheduler, which lets you define all maintenance routines within a single file. We will learn how to integrate Laravel Scheduler with Linux cron by setting up a dedicated cron entry that checks and executes scheduled tasks every minute. We will also learn how to create custom Artisan commands for things like clearing log files, generating reports, and archiving media files. We will also learn how to keep an eye on and fix any issues that pop up, using tools like Laravel Telescope and Debugbar. This'll make sure your backups and automated routines run smoothly, even when you're under a lot of pressure. The goal of this chapter is to give you the skills you need to automate repetitive tasks, cut down on manual interventions, and keep your application's integrity and performance high through a thorough automation plan.

Recipe 1: Combining Laravel Scheduler with Cron Jobs

There are several routine tasks—such as clearing logs, running periodic report generations, and refreshing cache data, which with time becomes a burden on your development team when executed manually. So, to streamline these tasks and ensure they run automatically, you may leverage Laravel's Scheduler in conjunction with Linux cron. By doing so, you can centralize all recurring tasks within Laravel and delegate their execution to a single cron entry on your Linux server. This integration ensures that scheduled tasks are automated reliably without duplicating installation procedures or requiring manual intervention.

Linking Laravel Scheduler with Linux Cron

The Laravel Scheduler allows you to define all your scheduled tasks in one place, in the **App\Console\Kernel.php** file, and then have them run automatically by triggering the **schedule:run** command every minute. This centralized approach reduces the complexity of managing multiple cron entries.

Configuring Scheduler in Kernel

- Open the **Kernel.php** file

Here, first navigate to your Laravel project's **app/Console/Kernel.php** file. Within the **schedule()** method, you can define all the scheduled tasks for "myapp." For instance, suppose you want to clear application logs daily; you can add a schedule definition as follows:

```
protected function schedule(Schedule $schedule)
```

```
{
    // Clear logs daily at midnight.
    $schedule->command('logs:clear')->daily();
    // Generate summary reports every Monday at 8 AM.
    $schedule->command('reports:generate')->weeklyOn(1,
'8:00');
    // Run a custom closure-based task every thirty minutes.
    $schedule->call(function () {
        // For example, refresh cache or update a dashboard.
        \Log::info('Cache refreshed at ' . now());
    })->everyThirtyMinutes();
}
```

In the above, the **logs:clear** command is scheduled to run daily at midnight, and the **reports:generate** command is set to run every Monday at 8 AM. Additionally, a closure-based task is scheduled every thirty minutes. These definitions centralize your recurring tasks in one file, making it easier to manage and adjust their frequencies as needed.

Setting up Linux Cron Job

Once you have defined your tasks in the **schedule()** method, the next step is to configure a single cron entry on your Linux server that runs the Laravel Scheduler command every minute. For this, run the following command in your Linux terminal while in the project directory, or navigate to your user's crontab:

```
crontab -e
```

Next, insert the following cron entry into the file:

```
* * * * * cd /path/to/myapp && php artisan schedule:run >>
/dev/null 2>&1
```

This cron entry executes the **php artisan schedule:run** command every minute. The command checks your schedule in Kernel.php and runs any tasks that are due at that moment. Save the changes to the crontab file, so as to have the daemon to trigger Laravel's Scheduler automatically.

Let's explore two practical examples that demonstrate this automation.

Example 1: Clearing Application Logs Daily

Suppose your application generates significant log files that need to be cleared periodically to conserve disk space. You might have a custom Artisan command to clear logs, such as **`logs:clear`**. In the Scheduler's **`schedule()`** method, you already defined:

```
$schedule->command('logs:clear')->daily();
```

To verify that the command works, you can run it manually:

```
php artisan logs:clear
```

Here, it confirms that log files in **`storage/logs`** are deleted or rotated as intended.

At midnight, the cron entry triggers **`php artisan schedule:run`**. The Scheduler then checks and runs the **`logs:clear`** command. You can verify its execution by inspecting your Laravel logs or by checking the file system for the absence of old logs.

Example 2: Generating Weekly Summary Reports

Lets say that your application needs to compile and send a summary report every Monday at 8 AM. You have implemented an Artisan command called **`reports:generate`**. In the Scheduler configuration, you add:

```
$schedule->command('reports:generate')->weeklyOn(1, '8:00');
```

Test the command manually by running:

```
php artisan reports:generate
```

We need to make sure that the summary report is generated and stored/sent as expected. On Monday at 8:00, the Scheduler sees that the **`reports:generate`** command is due. With the cron job running every minute, Laravel Scheduler triggers the report generation automatically. And post-execution, you can verify the process by checking the generated reports in your designated storage or by reviewing email logs if the report is emailed.

Recipe 2: Automating Database Backups and Recovery Routines

Let's say our app is coupled with multiple database model. It may happen that we face a critical challenge: with multiple databases and increasing data volumes, the critical data need to be backed up consistently and on schedule. And, the risk of data loss due to server failures, accidental deletions, or other unforeseen issues may push us to implement an automated backup system. So here, you will learn to automate these database backups and recovery routines—ensuring that backups run reliably at scheduled intervals with minimal manual oversight, while also integrating processes for recovery when necessary. This process will be demonstrated using the Spatie Laravel Backup package along with Laravel Scheduler and Linux cron commands.

Installing and Configuring Backup Package

To automate database backups in Laravel, we will utilize the popular **Spatie Laravel Backup** package. If not already installed, open your Linux terminal in the "myapp" directory and run:

```
composer require spatie/laravel-backup
```

Next, publish the configuration file using Artisan:

```
php artisan vendor:publish --
provider="Spatie\Backup\BackupServiceProvider"
```

This command creates a configuration file at **config/backup.php**, where you can define what files, directories, and databases to backup, such as:

- **'backup' => ['name' => env('APP_NAME', 'laravel-backup'), ...]** – This sets a unique name.
- **'source' => ['files' => ['include' => [base_path()], 'exclude' => ['vendor', 'node_modules'], ...], 'databases' => ['mysql'],],** – This specifies which directories and databases should be backed up.

If your project uses multiple database connections, list them in the **'databases'** array.

Setting up Automated Backups

With the backup configuration in place, integrate the backup routine into your automated task pipeline using Laravel Scheduler. To do this, open **app/Console/Kernel.php** and define a new scheduled task within the **schedule()** method as shown below:

```
protected function schedule(Schedule $schedule)
{
    // Run backups daily at 2 AM.
    $schedule->command('backup:run --only-db')-
>dailyAt('02:00');
```

```
    // Alternatively, to backup both databases and files, you can use:
    // $schedule->command('backup:run')->dailyAt('02:00');
}
```

This line instructs Laravel to trigger the backup command every day at 2 AM using the **backup:run** Artisan command. If you choose **--only-db**, only the databases specified in your **config/backup.php** are backed up; omit it to backup both databases and file storage as defined.

Creating and Testing Backup Routine

While the Laravel Scheduler will run the scheduled tasks if your cron is correctly set up, you need to make sure that Laravel's Scheduler itself is triggered every minute by running:

```
crontab -e
```

Then add the following entry:

```
* * * * * cd /path/to/myapp && php artisan schedule:run >> /dev/null 2>&1
```

This cron entry calls **php artisan schedule:run** every minute to evaluate and execute scheduled tasks at the appropriate time.

Implementing Recovery Routines

Now the recovery plan is also equally important compared to the backup plan. The Spatie Laravel Backup package provides instructions on how to restore backups. Here, the recovery is typically a manual process in production environments.

So, to restore a backup, first we have to identify the backup file from the backups directory. And then, use your database's command-line tools (like **mysql** for MySQL) to restore the database as shown below:

```
mysql -u your_username -p your_database < /path/to/backup-file.sql
```

For files, simply copy the backup files back to their required locations.

This automated routine really cut down on manual intervention, made sure your data was always protected, and offered a solid recovery strategy for keeping your data intact in a high-traffic, multi-database environment.

Recipe 3: Configuring Custom Task Automation Scripts

While Laravel Scheduler is very well handling the standard tasks very efficiently, there will be instances where you need more specialized automation scripts. Some tasks may require the use of custom shell commands that could perform specific actions not natively covered by Laravel's Artisan commands such as complex file manipulations, running system-level maintenance operations, or executing third-party utility commands that complement your Laravel operations. So here, we need a flexible system, one that could run custom shell scripts and integrate their execution within the Laravel command infrastructure. We are now going to learn how to design and execute custom shell scripts and integrate them with Laravel commands. It will provide you with the capability to automate unique and complex tasks with ease while keeping all automated processes organized and consistent.

Creating Custom Shell Script

First, let's create a custom shell script that performs a unique task. For our demonstration, imagine you need a script that archives old images from your media directory into a compressed file for backup or cleanup purposes.

First, create a file called **archive_images.sh**:

```
nano archive_images.sh
```

In the editor, simply input the following script:

```
#!/bin/bash
# Define the source and target directories.
SOURCE_DIR="storage/app/media"
BACKUP_DIR="storage/app/backup/images"
TIMESTAMP=$(date +"%Y%m%d_%H%M%S")
ARCHIVE_FILE="$BACKUP_DIR/images_backup_$TIMESTAMP.tar.gz"
# Create the backup directory if it doesn't exist.
mkdir -p "$BACKUP_DIR"
# Create a compressed archive of the media files.
tar -czf "$ARCHIVE_FILE" -C "$SOURCE_DIR" .
# Optionally, delete the archived files from the source
directory after archiving.
```

```
# rm -rf "$SOURCE_DIR"/*
echo "Images archived to $ARCHIVE_FILE"
```

This above script does the following:

- It sets the source directory as your media directory and the backup directory where the archives will be stored.
- It generates a timestamp to ensure that backup filenames are unique.
- It creates the backup directory if it doesn't already exist.
- It creates a compressed archive of all files in the media directory.
- Optionally, the script can delete the original files after archiving by uncommenting the deletion line.
- Finally, it echoes a confirmation message.

Integrating Shell Script with Laravel Commands

Next, we then integrate the shell script execution into your Laravel environment by creating a custom Artisan command that will invoke the shell script as below:

```
php artisan make:command ArchiveImages
```

This generates a new command class located at **`app/Console/Commands/ArchiveImages.php`**. Then open the **`ArchiveImages.php`** in PhpStorm and modify it as follows:

```
<?php
namespace App\Console\Commands;
use Illuminate\Console\Command;
use Symfony\Component\Process\Process;
class ArchiveImages extends Command
{
    /**
     * The name and signature of the console command.
     *
     * @var string
     */
```

```
    protected $signature = 'images:archive';
    /**
     * The console command description.
     *
     * @var string
     */
    protected $description = 'Archive old images from the
media directory to a compressed file.';
    /**
     * Execute the console command.
     *
     * @return int
     */
    public function handle()
    {
        $this->info('Starting image archival process...');
        // Define the script path relative to the project root
        $scriptPath = base_path('archive_images.sh');
        // Ensure the script exists.
        if (!file_exists($scriptPath)) {
            $this->error('The archive_images.sh script was not
found.');
            return 1;
        }
        // Create a Symfony Process to execute the shell
script
        $process = new Process(["bash", $scriptPath]);
        $process->setTimeout(300); // Set timeout to 5 minutes
if needed
        try {
            $process->run();
```

```
            // Check if the process executed successfully
            if (!$process->isSuccessful()) {
                $this->error('Error during archival: ' .
$process->getErrorOutput());
                return 1;
            }
            // Output the script's output to the console
            $this->info($process->getOutput());
        } catch (\Exception $e) {
            $this->error('Exception occurred: ' . $e-
>getMessage());
            return 1;
        }
        $this->info('Image archival process completed
successfully.');
        return 0;
    }
}
```

The above script uses the Symfony Process component to execute your shell script. The command checks for the existence of the script, runs it, and handles any errors by logging them to the console.

Scheduling Custom Artisan Command

Once your custom Artisan command is ready, within the **schedule()** method, add an entry to run your command at a desired frequency. For example, to run the archival script daily at 3 AM:

```
protected function schedule(Schedule $schedule)
{
    // Schedule the image archival process to run daily at 3
AM
    $schedule->command('images:archive')->dailyAt('03:00');
```

```
}
```

This configuration ensures that the **images:archive** command is executed automatically by Laravel's Scheduler without any manual intervention. With the above detailed steps, you successfully configured custom task automation scripts integrated with Laravel commands for our app.

Recipe 4: Generating Scheduled Analytical Reports

During your performance reviews and team planning sessions, you came across an opportunity that timely, analytical reports could provide valuable insights such as trends in user activity, order statistics, content engagement, and database performance. However, manually generating these reports was time-consuming and error-prone. To streamline this process, you decided to automate analytical report generation using Laravel's Scheduler. With this setup, your application would periodically process key data, compile it into an analytical summary, and either store it for further inspection or send it directly to stakeholders. So here, you will learn how to create a custom Artisan command to generate these scheduled reports and integrate it with the Laravel Scheduler to facilitate the automated production of analytical summaries without interrupting your daily operations.

Creating Custom Artisan Command for Report Generation

The first step is to generate a new Artisan command using Laravel's built-in command generator, which we can do by running the following command:

```
php artisan make:command GenerateAnalyticalReport
```

This command creates a new file at **app/Console/Commands/GenerateAnalyticalReport.php**. Next, open the generated file and you will see a basic command template. Just update it to include the logic for generating your analytical report and the command will perform database queries, process the data, and store the resulting report in a designated folder.

Following is a quick example:

```
<?php
namespace App\Console\Commands;
use Illuminate\Console\Command;
use Illuminate\Support\Facades\DB;
```

```
use Illuminate\Support\Facades\File;
class GenerateAnalyticalReport extends Command
{
    /**
     * The name and signature of the console command.
     *
     * @var string
     */
    protected $signature = 'report:generate';
    /**
     * The console command description.
     *
     * @var string
     */
    protected $description = 'Generate an analytical summary
of application data and store it in a report file';
    /**
     * Execute the console command.
     *
     * @return int
     */
    public function handle()
    {
        $this->info('Starting report generation...');
        // Fetch data for the report; for example, get user
registration count and post totals.
        $totalUsers = DB::table('users')->count();
        $newUsers = DB::table('users')->where('created_at',
'>=', now()->subWeek())->count();
        $totalPosts = DB::table('posts')->count();
```

```
        $postsLastWeek = DB::table('posts')-
>where('created_at', '>=', now()->subWeek())->count();
        $averagePostsPerUser = $totalUsers > 0 ?
round($totalPosts / $totalUsers, 2) : 0;
        // You can add more complex metrics as needed.
        $data = [
            'Total Users' => $totalUsers,
            'New Users (last week)' => $newUsers,
            'Total Posts' => $totalPosts,
            'Posts in Last Week' => $postsLastWeek,
            'Average Posts Per User' => $averagePostsPerUser,
            'Report Generated At' => now()-
>toDateTimeString(),
        ];
        // Format the report text
        $reportContent = "Analytical Report for myapp\n";
        $reportContent .=
"===================================\n\n";
        foreach ($data as $key => $value) {
            $reportContent .= "$key: $value\n";
        }
        // Define the directory and filename for the report
        $reportDir = storage_path('app/reports');
        if (!File::exists($reportDir)) {
            File::makeDirectory($reportDir, 0755, true);
        }
        $filename = 'report_' . now()->format('Ymd_His') .
'.txt';
        $reportPath = $reportDir . '/' . $filename;
        // Write the report to a file
        File::put($reportPath, $reportContent);
```

```
        $this->info("Report generated successfully:
{$reportPath}");
        return 0;
    }
}
```

In the above example, the command:

- Counts total users, new users within the last week, total posts, and posts created in the last week.
- Calculates an average metric for user engagement.
- Formats these data points into a structured text report.
- Stores the report in a dedicated **reports** directory inside **storage/app/reports**.
- Outputs a success message to the console.

Scheduling Report Generation Command

With the custom command ready, integrate it into Laravel's Scheduler so that it runs automatically at specified intervals. Open **app/Console/Kernel.php** in PhpStorm. Within the **schedule()** method, add an entry for your new command. For example, to run the report generation daily at 4 AM, update the method as follows:

```
protected function schedule(Schedule $schedule)
{
    // Schedule the analytical report generation to run daily
at 4 AM.
    $schedule->command('report:generate')->dailyAt('04:00');
    // You can schedule other tasks here as needed.
}
```

This instructs Laravel Scheduler to check every minute whether any scheduled tasks are due. At 4 AM, Laravel will execute the **report:generate** command automatically, producing the report without any manual intervention.

Summary

Throughout this chapter, you worked around the automation of routine operations in your app by integrating Laravel Scheduler with Linux cron. You configured the Scheduler within the `Kernel.php` file and defined recurring tasks, such as clearing logs and generating summary reports, ensuring these maintenance processes were executed automatically without manual intervention. You created custom Artisan commands, like the one for generating analytical reports, that aggregated key metrics and stored the resulting data for further analysis. Additionally, you linked Laravel's scheduling with Linux cron by setting up a single cron entry, which triggered **`php artisan schedule:run`** every minute.

In combination with monitoring tools like Laravel Telescope, Debugbar, and standard Linux utilities in this entire book, your approach ensured that maintenance operations did not overwhelm the system and that performance remained optimal, effectively preparing your app for scalability and high-traffic usage.

Index

U

V

Epilogue

After working through all the recipes, I'm amazed at what I see beyond just code snippets and commands. I see the moments when a failing migration stopped me in my tracks—and the confidence I gained when I applied eager loading to eliminate dozens of hidden queries. I saw firsthand how wrestling with an elusive authentication bug can lead to breakthroughs, especially when you grasp the power of middleware and two-factor flows. I remember nights spent chasing down why a background job never fired, then waking to the simple truth of a missing queue worker. The challenges I've faced have taught me that troubleshooting isn't a sign of failure, but a stepping stone to true mastery. The path you've just walked is one that many have taken before you, and you've now joined their ranks. You've learned to inspect your environment, lock down permissions, and confirm that every artisan command behaves exactly as expected. You've traced dynamic routes from URL to controller, watched Blade render nested data structures, and caught the subtle mistakes that lead to N+1 problems. You've set breakpoints in your mind—knowing where validation rules live, where exceptions get reported, and where notifications flow. You've seen how a misconfigured scheduler or a silent job failure can ripple through an application, and you've fixed it on the spot.

I'm thrilled to tell you that debugging is no longer a frustrating guesswork exercise! You have an incredible toolbox at your disposal: Laravel Debugbar and Telescope are here to reveal what happens under the hood; log channels and Pulse alerts will bring errors to your attention in real time; queued job retry strategies will recover from transient network hiccups; and automated backups will ensure you can always roll back when things go awry. It's like you have X-ray vision when it comes to reading the signs—like when you spot a spike in query time, an unauthorized 403 response, or a stalled cron job. And you always know exactly which recipe to reach for, like a pro!

The more you troubleshoot, the more you'll recognize patterns. You'll start to see things like a missing foreign key, an unregistered middleware, a stale cache entry, or an expired API token. Through dedicated practice, you've mastered fixing each of these in isolation and in combination. You've built confidence in your ability to dissect a problem, test a hypothesis, and apply a targeted solution. And because each recipe built on the last, you never lost your place or repeated work you'd already mastered. And as you move forward, you'll encounter new challenges—integrating third-party services, scaling under heavy load, adapting to new Laravel features. When those moments arrive, remember that every bug is an invitation to learn. With the same investigative spirit you brought to these recipes, you're sure to find the answers you need. Just inspect your logs, step through your code, consult your mental index of patterns, and apply the precise fix. You'll solve the immediate issue and gain a deeper understanding of how Laravel works.

The key to building a strong and resilient development process is troubleshooting! With the amazing techniques and recipes you've absorbed, you'll face every error message with curiosity instead of dread. You'll diagnose problems quickly, correct them confidently, and keep your applications running smoothly. This book is a must-read! It's packed with insights that will transform the way you look at errors. No matter where your Laravel journey takes you, you can always count on one thing: you'll never be stopped by a bug!

Thank You

www.ingramcontent.com/pod-product-compliance
Lightning Source LLC
Chambersburg PA
CBHW080216170726
48282CB00030B/1135
9789349174351